MW01109615

# SIRIUS-LY RICH

## A TRIBUTE TO THE CITY OF CLEVELAND, OHIO, THE BRIGHTEST STAR IN THE NORTHERN HEMISPHERE

*Blessings one Wandey, a very bright star in our "forever" galaxy!*

*Enjoy! w/ love.*

## JANE SUTPHIN LEITCH

*Gratefully yours,*
*Jane S. L.*

Lulu Publishing Services rev. date: 10/28/2015

# DEDICATION

To my very special sisters and brothers

In fondest memory:
Mary E., Carolyn and Jimmy

For:
Alberta and Cal

Our brother, our brother

Jimmy Hoynes Sutphin died on May 8, 2015, just before his 83$^{rd}$ birthday on May 28, 2015.

Three events – not heretofore mentioned – are his legacy:

1. He jogged a segment of the 26-mile run before the 2002 Winter Olympics games, carrying the torch to Columbus, Ohio, for his country.
2. The Rotary Club of his city, Hudson, Ohio, designated March 26 – forever – "Jimmy Sutphin Day" as an award for "Service Above Self."
3. He was President of Braden Sutphin Ink from 1968 to 1984 – the oldest family-owned ink company in the country.

His mantra (from our Dad): "The greatest sin is that of ungratefulness!"

# PROLOGUE

# SIRIUS-LY RICH

A salute to our own Cleveland, Ohio, U.S.A. – the
brightest star in the Northern Hemisphere

We don't want our own "stars" to be dimmed in the rich universe of our "home town," Cleveland, Ohio.

If you love city history, you will want to remember a daring young man who borrowed $1,000,000 on his signature at the height of the Depression (1934) to build an ice palace for a defunct hockey team he had just purchased and to bring a bright light to his home town.

He was 40 years old!

His wife, 37 years old, is also noteworthy because she didn't leave him or cry a lot. She just recited her rosary beads, loved him and their six children, and believed in his hard-work ethic and in divine intervention.

They are Albert Claude Sutphin and Mary Althea Hoynes Sutphin.

Their six children are: Mary Elizabeth, Florence Jane, Carolyn Alberta, Alberta Ernestine, James Hoynes, and Albert Carleton.

The Zutphen family from Zutphen, Holland, The Netherlands, arrived in New Amsterdam (New York City) in the late 1700s.

The Hoynes (O'Hayne) family of ten brothers from Gavin, West Ireland, found themselves at Ellis Island, escaping the potato famine of 1845. They are Sirius-ly rich because of a very special Place, because of those who brought them to this Place, and because of the lessons they have learned there – as a family!

In the 1920s, Albert and Mary Sutphin become the teachers of many lessons.

Albert thrives on hard work at his Braden Sutphin Ink Company and at all sports.

Mary thrives on rearing their six children and keeping up with Albert.

The children thrive in belonging to a family where chances are taken, interesting duties are assigned (some even followed), and rules leaving no doubt about obeying your elders.

In 1934, in the dining room of their house on Derbyshire Road in Cleveland Heights, Mary is presented with the challenge of her life and her marriage. It is here that Albert confesses to his purchase of a defunct ice hockey team from an acquaintance named Happy "Hap" Holmes.

He follows this shocker in 1936 with the news of the $1,000,000 debt he has taken on to build the sports palace that will bring prosperity to Cleveland. It will seat thousands of happy fans. The team is now named "The Falcons." Terms of the loan: There must be 300 other events a year – not just hockey.

Albert will limit his duties at his beloved printing ink company and become the booking agent for many diverse attractions at the new ice palace. He will spend weeks on the road putting acts together, booking circuses, rodeos, six-day bike races, aquaramas, ice shows, and, of course, thirty home and thirty away hockey games, and, eventually, professional basketball.

Albert confesses it is because he loves Cleveland – his hometown where his family will live, be educated, grow up, and marry – Clevelanders!

He believes his efforts at building an all-events arena during the crushing Depression, with soup kitchens downtown, will also bring hope to this hurting Place.

Mary worries: If this is her life now, she wants to stop the world, and when the world stops, she needs to get off!

In the stopped world, the gypsies do not come to pick dandelions in the spring. Spang Bakery will not deliver fresh bread and donuts. We cannot hear the ragman holler, "Papah! Rags!," or the scissors grinder's bell. Even the ice man doesn't cometh, nor does a poor soul come asking for a meal at the back door.

And what did Albert do?

He was scared to death!

Crushing hard work and Mary's prayers prevailed.

He paid back every penny!!

All investors took home three times their original investment when Al Sutphin sold the Arena twelve years later, in 1949.

In the twelve years of running Arena operations, Sutphin took home a salary of $1.00 a year.

The investors earned yearly interest on their debentures bonds.

Albert had taken out a second mortgage on their family home for $25,000. He and all investors with similar investments of $25,000 took home $75,000. It was 1949. Albert had never had so much money.


LESSON: TAKE TIME TO WORK AND PRAY; IT GUARANTEES SUCCESS.

Our on-going story – and the lessons to be learned – will be taught in decades on our journey together.

Your attention please!

The bus is waiting. School is starting. Thank you for coming to class.

Blessings, Florence Jane Sutphin-Leitch

Written for: Mary E., Carolyn, Alberta, Jimmy, and Cal – the best siblings ever! – and with love and wonder for our twenty-eight children.

P.S.: Jane feels her family story of love and courage – even daring – is an essential part of her favorite city's historical past.

In this exciting time of Cleveland's "renaissance" – sparked by the hosting of the 2016 G.O.P. National Convention – the Sutphin family is still here, 72 strong, and growing a lot!

The family company, Braden Sutphin Ink, has had 102 anniversaries in their Cleveland company headquarters at E. 93rd and Aetna Avenue. The Sutphin family and over 150 employees represent and foster the same love that Albert and Mary Hoynes Sutphin felt for their home town.

# CHAPTER I

# THE 1900s – 1920s

Our first lesson starts on a high note:

> "Take the time to love and be loved – it is a God-given privilege."

Albert Claude Sutphin is joined in the holy sacrament of matrimony with Mary Althea Hoynes – and the angels sing!

It is August 14, 1922. St. Philomena's Catholic Church in East Cleveland, Ohio, welcomes Albert's devout Presbyterian family and Mary's Irish Catholic (lively) revelers.

Albert is home after WWI. He has served with the 135th Field Artillery Battery "D" in the trenches in Pierrefitte (near Metz), France, a farm community where your wealth is determined by the size of the manure pile in your front yard.

They return to France – Paris – for their honeymoon. Post-war Paris is not the wild R and R of Albert's war years; but, for them, Paris – even in August – is springtime!

Next, they arrange a reunion in Pierrefitte with Pierre Gillot and his family. Pierre, Al Sutphin's age – also eighteen – had jumped into the trenches to join the American Expeditionary Forces, and the two soldiers became close buddies. Albert learns that Pierre's family owns the only "Café du Commerce" in Pierrefitte. Albert's luck just keeps going! Their fellow soldiers soon understand Pierre's inherent value – he will run home and steal chickens and return to the trenches to cook them in their helmets!

Post-war inflation has done as much damage to Europe as the French 75s (a huge cannon).

They travel on to Germany. In Berlin, Albert buys Mary a pony-skin fur coat. He brings the money in a large suitcase. Fifty American dollars is 2800 Deutschmarks.

Albert and Mary are 28 and 26 years old. He was born in Franklin, Ohio, on April 11, 1894. She was born in Akron, Ohio, on June 21, 1896. No one is hiding their ages!

Albert's parents are Carleton Ernest Sutphin and Elizabeth Pearl Thayer – both born in Middletown, Ohio.

Ernest came to Cleveland in the early 1900s to accept a sales position with the Central Ohio Paper Company. He was so serious about it – he stayed for 50 years, and loved every minute of it!

He had three sisters: Carrie, Edna, and Ethel, all members of the Daughters of the American Revolution. William Sutphin fought in the American Revolution from his home in New Jersey.

Ernie's wife, Elizabeth, was the oldest of eight – all the household duties fell upon her. She escaped at sixteen, married nineteen-year-old Ernie, and gave birth to their one and only son, Albert.

Mary's parents are Michael Hoynes and Florence Melvina Brownell.

Florence's father, Oscar Brownell, was a physician who served on the battlefields of the Civil War. He took little Florence to a political rally in Springfield, Illinois. She waved to Abraham Lincoln, which made her famous in the family at 11 months of age.

Florence's mother was born in Alsace Lorraine – French and German – with strong ideals of hard work and love of family.

Michael and Florence have five children.

Florence is the oldest; she is a talented artist, with beautiful red hair.

She was followed by Daniel, a wild and loving Irishman – as dozens of friends would attest – especially his pals in Cleveland's police and fire brigades. Daniel was known to ring false fire alarms – then play poker when the firefighters arrived.

Our mother, Mary Althea, was next. She was the only Hoynes with deep brown eyes and chestnut brown hair – definitely French and German traits.

Mary is followed by two younger brothers, Paul and Denis. They played tricks pretending to be twins and fooling people.

Denis became an attorney. He joined his family business, Central Electrotype, rather than a law firm. Paul took care of Central's front office.

Albert's parents are Presbyterian. Every Sunday, they attend three services at Forest Hills Presbyterian Church in Cleveland Heights.

Mary's parents are devout Roman Catholics. Her mother converted to Catholicism when she married Michael Hoynes. They attend St. Edward "Irish" Catholic Church on Woodland Avenue. A block away is St. Joseph "German" Catholic Church – never to be confused – the Irish leave their bars open on Sunday!

The Temperance Ladies begin forming!

By the time the Hoyneses and the Sutphins realize that Albert is a serious suitor for their beloved daughter, any objections have been overcome. After all, Albert is hard working and good looking – he has a way about him – as Mary will find out.

There is something about Mary – her kindness, patience, her sense of duty and Irish humor – that can make this marriage work.

Albert has a very big decision to make. He cannot marry a Roman Catholic without promising to bring up the children as baptized Catholics and educated in Catholic schools.

Albert agrees to all conditions!

Mary embarks on a life she instinctively understands and wins medals for patience and perseverance.

Albert wins Mary's undying love and appreciation for a life never imagined by either one of them.

LESSON: LOVE'S LABOR IS NEVER LOST!

Albert is a very hard-working ink manufacturer and salesman for the Braden Ink Company on E. 22<sup>nd</sup> Street (now property of Cleveland State University).

Mary's father, Michael Hoynes, has taken a leap of faith to create the Central Electrotype Company – also on E. 22$^{nd}$ Street. Years later, his sons join him; and Mary serves as a summer receptionist.

To raise the money for this endeavor, Michael and Florence have opened a boarding house. They clean and cook for long hard hours to make their boarders happy and their company happen.

Albert – with that way about him – got lucky. He was riding on a streetcar in April of his senior year at Central High School. He was seated beside a prosperous-looking man. As they shared a seat and became acquainted, there was something about Albert's business goals and ambition that caused Jim Braden to say, "I need a sharp young man to come to work for me on Monday. Albert answers, "I'm your man!" That "Monday" became a lifetime at the Braden (later, "and Sutphin") Ink Company.

Albert never returned to Central High, nor graduated. Years later, he couldn't join the University Club – next door to the Arena – because he hadn't attended college.

Remembering his war years, he did, however, during the six months it took to build the Arena, live in a rustic shack on Chester Avenue in a vacant lot.

He loved it!

It was destroyed by fire – probably started by one of Albert's El Verso cigars. All of his papers and records were destroyed.

He moved home and adjusted!

**LESSON: WAR AND THE TRENCHES IN FRANCE CAN BE A GREAT TRAINING GROUND.**

The Braden Ink Company and Central Electrotype were just three doors apart on E. 22$^{nd}$ Street in downtown Cleveland. The summer that Mary Hoynes began working for her father, she was introduced to a go-getter who sold ink to him.

His name was Albert Sutphin, star athlete on local sports teams – baseball all spring and summer, football all fall, and ice hockey (out-of-doors) all winter.

Mary, when not working for her father, helped her mother at home, supervising her two challenging younger brothers and serving the boarders.

The two companies complement one another. Albert sold ink to Central, and Central makes "blankets" for Braden. ("Blankets" are a cloth-backed rubber wrap around a metal cylinder which delivers ink to the paper.)

To further family ties, the trenches in France found Dan Hoynes (Mary's oldest brother) and Albert Sutphin soldiers together with the 135th Field Artillery.

Dan's eyesight was questionable, and he lied about his skills and volunteered as a cook – to constant complaints – and indigestion. (Thirty years later, his son, Jimmy Hoynes, lied about his age, and volunteered in the U. S. Navy in World War II.)

Albert remembers his father as a tough Dutch taskmaster. He reared him to be financially independent and self-reliant.

Albert's first job was polishing drills in a factory. He was ten years old and hated the monotony of the job. When they changed the size of the drills, every bored worker cheered.

With his first earnings, he bought a bicycle. He put the neighbor's laundry in a basket on the handlebars, and peddled seven miles to a laundry near Euclid Beach Park. Albert soon realized he would always need to be the "Boss" and find work that challenged him.

Albert and Mary travelled in very different social circles.

Albert's friends knew sandlots, football fields and frozen ice rinks in public parks.

Mary was popular at Notre Dame Academy near her home, she and her friends attended the "Easter Monday Ball" – bigger than New Year's Eve – and her dates were always polite, well-mannered Catholic young gentlemen. (Don't laugh!)

LESSON: TAKE TIME TO PLAY. IT IS THE SECRET OF YOUTH AND WELL-BEING.

Being married brought new challenges!
Four little girls were born in the next five years:

| | |
|---|---|
| (Leader) Mary Elizabeth | 1923 |
| Florence Jane | 1925 |
| Carolyn Alberta | 1926 |

Alberta Ernestine          1928

There is a problem! They are all girls! Albert can't imagine this! He asks, "Who will play sports with me? Who will carry on the family name? Who will follow me in the business?" These are vital concerns to a sports-loving and serious entrepreneur-in-the-making!

## LESSON: TAKE TIME TO LAUGH – IT IS THE MUSIC OF THE SOUL.

Albert can't laugh! He worries! There is a Great Depression – caused by the stock market crash the year after Alberta is born.

It seemed hopeless to keep on speculating, but Albert is unglued:

> "Girls need a lot of things."
> "They marry and move away."
> "The grandchildren will live out of town."
> "I'll very rarely visit with them."
> "I'll never be an influence on them."
> "I'll never be their 'Champ.'"

The children have been baptized at St. Ann's Church, Pastor John Mary Powers presiding. Soon, they will attend St. Ann School, where the Ursuline nuns rule. They are outstanding teachers and great disciplinarians, who instill lessons to live by:

1. Love of learning!
2. Obedience to faith and family!
3. Sacrifices won't kill you!
4. March in the halls without talking, or you will have to report to the principal's office!

## LESSON: TO HAVE FAITH IS TO HAVE WINGS. (J. M. BARRIE)

Albert eases up!

The girls laughingly believe he has forgiven them for causing the stock market crash when Alberta was one year old.

He finds himself enjoying Saturday morning's game of "Rough and Tumble" with four little laughing preschoolers and Sunday nights with Eddie Cantor and The Texaco Hour. No words were allowed in a room lit only by firelight – if you talked, you were sent to bed!

When playing Rough and Tumble, Mary, Jane, Carolyn and Alberta want Daddy to be a big bear. They will jump all over him and push him around. They dance, whooping and hollering. Daddy pretends to be afraid, so he roars a lot; but soon he is fast asleep on the living room floor. The children are delighted. They have killed the big, noisy bear; and now they can mess with his hair.

Daddy wears his hair parted in the middle. When he wakes up, it will be parted on the side. Daddy pretends not to recognize himself, and staggers around the room. The girls clap and cheer!

Here is a Dad – before huge financial responsibility took over – who was our Mom's devoted family partner. He changed diapers, did the laundry, ran errands, and drove us to church!

## LESSON: LOVE BEGINS AT HOME. (MOTHER THERESA)

Wanting a namesake, Albert is dumbfounded when his first-born, Mary Elizabeth, isn't Albert Claude Sutphin, Junior.

However, Albert's mother, Elizabeth Pearl is delighted! She proudly delivered Albert Claude, and now she has a grandchild – a *girl*!

Gramma Hoynes had her first grandchild two years earlier – a boy named Daniel. (Many years later, he became little Florence Jane Sutphin's godfather.)

As soon as Mary E. could talk, she named Gramma Sutphin "Sutton" and Grampa Sutphin "Gaga." They were never called anything else by the family.

When Mary E. was old enough, she became a regular guest on week-ends at Lynn Park Drive in Cleveland Heights. (Gaga and Sutton had moved there from 64th and Woodland when Albert and Mary were married.)

Mary E. always returned home wearing a big starched bow in her hair, lots of new fancy dresses, and doll babies with pretty outfits.

By the time Mary E. is seven, she has traded in her fussy dresses for slacks, her dolls for tools, and has established a lemonade stand on the tree lawn in the front yard – acting every bit like the Junior Albert Sutphin was looking for.

Still anticipating a male heir, a second child is born just fifteen months later.

Unable to explain another girl, Florence Jane's engraved birth announcement – sent to many family, friends and business associates – reads as follows:

Red Grange – the Galloping Ghost rushed for 32 touchdowns.
Babe Ruth – hit 30 home runs and 21 RBIs.
Johnny Weissmuller – broke the 1924 Olympic record for the 100 meter in 58.6 seconds.
But Florence Jane, born February 18, 1925, will never know about these things. Girls are like that!

Footnote: Those athletic records are *1924* data.

Red Grange's real name was Harold Edwards. Babe Ruth's lifetime record was 714 home runs and 2,213 RBIs.

Jane, determined to win him over, fostered love and awe for her Dad's accomplishments. She sat at his end of the family dinner table – putting pepper on everything – just as he did. She made sure that there was double butter on his nightly popcorn, and plenty of ice water – whenever he wanted it.

Jane's first big lesson comes at six years of age. She is sharing the only bathroom with her Dad. He is shaving to go to work. Jane is dressing for her second day of first grade at St. Ann School.

Daddy asks, "Jane, what did you learn in school yesterday?"

Jane is thrilled to have a grown-up conversation.

She responds, "Oh, Daddy, I learned that boys have wieners!"

Albert is stunned! He angrily towels off the shaving cream and goes looking for Jane's mother.

Jane is confused! Why would her Daddy not be interested in this enlightening information?

There was an uncomfortable conversation about the value of Catholic school education.

## LESSON: YOU CAN'T TELL YOUR PARENTS ANYTHING – UNTIL THEY GROW UP.

No one is surprised when the next baby, Carolyn Alberta, is another girl.

It's a habit!

Everyone *is* surprised – especially her Dad – when she proves to be an outstanding athlete.

The year that St. Ann's built a tennis court, Carolyn took on all comers, and just kept winning – all summer long.

At Laurel School, she was elected to the "All-City Girls' Field Hockey Team."

At graduation, she was awarded the Laurel "L" for outstanding achievement in Leadership, Scholarship, and Athletics.

The fourth – our Dad was numb – and final girl, Alberta Ernestine, becomes an outstanding figure skater. She will be featured at all the Cleveland Arena's home hockey games, wearing a "Phillip Morris"-style red outfit – complete with that "bell boy" cap.

First, she arrives on a sled and performs her ten-minute skating routine – complete with her best "sit spin."

Next, she will present the "Lucky Number Winners" with gift certificates from the 98-page hockey program.

Just after opening night, she forgot to get on the sled, and it went out without her. How embarrassing was that – especially with a table lamp on the back to be raffled off to a lucky winner. Let's give her a break. She was only eight – and nervous!

Two years later, she skated her famous backward spiral – one leg high over her head – straight into the Barons' goalie cage that was left on the ice. To add insult to injury, the Barons hockey team got shut out that night. When Alberta arrived home, her sisters teased her unmercifully. She defended herself by saying, "Well, somebody made a goal tonight!"

The decade of the 1920s ends with the first clue that Albert Sutphin has ideas for "going places" that a Depression, a wife and four little daughters, and a very hurting home town can't discourage!

9

He buys the Braden Ink Company – Sutphin style – with the *honest* approach!

Jim Braden had become so caught up in African safaris with experienced explorer Martin Johnson, he was mostly absent during important decision-making times at the company.

Since Albert had become "acting boss" and loved it, he approached Mr. Braden with a proposition.

"I have no 'real' money – because of my big family – but I can make payments; and I would know how to grow this company, especially in sales, covering a much bigger territory – all over Ohio and the East."

Mr. Braden responded, "Tell you what, Albert, send me a check (a figure never disclosed), and I'll tell you when you have bought the company!"

Mr. Braden was killed in a plane accident, with Martin Johnson, seven years later. Albert sent a check – every month – to his widow, Eleanor, who lived to be 93 years young.

The amount has never been revealed – ever!

The decade of the 1930s is upon us, and – hold onto your hats – it's a doozy!

# CHAPTER II

# THE 1930S

The 1930s stretch all imagining for the Sutphin family – challenging, and scary, too.

The very first event doesn't scare anyone. James Hoynes Sutphin is born on May 28, 1932 – *a boy* – after four girls!

He is wildly welcomed!

Daddy can't stop smiling!

Mother marvels at how many differences there are.

The four sisters, Mary (10), Jane (8), Carolyn (6) and Alberta (4), sing, "A brother, a brother – no bother – we know everything to do!"

1. "We dress him in our doll clothes."
2. "We curl his hair."
3. "We give him extra toys, because he is a Prince."

Daddy just keeps smiling and sees Jimmy selling printing ink someday.

Mother hopes he'll sleep through the night – soon.

There are too many baseball gloves, footballs, hockey sticks, tennis racquets – Ben Gay – for one boy, so a second son is ordered up – seven years later – on August 16, 1939.

At 43 years, our mother has earned naming rights – for sure.

She proudly names him William "Thayer" (after Albert's mother), and she loves the idea of the new "Billy" having a brother, "Jimmy" – so boyish!

The christening will be celebrated at St. Ann Church, Father John Mary Powers presiding – as usual.

Mother stays home to prepare a reception. Albert returns, holding their new baby boy, and Mary reaches out for "Billy." Daddy says, "Mary, meet 'Albert Carleton,' named for my father and me."

Mary starts a novena for the future of her marriage.

LESSON: IF YOU ARE IRISH, SMILE, AND KEEP PRAYING; YOU HAVE 35 MORE YEARS TO GO!

With Jimmy's arrival, a special gift entered our lives to save our mother's very existence and to enrich every day for all of us – for the next six years.

Her name was Elizabeth "Betty" Cook. She was sixteen and newly emancipated from an orphanage – as was the norm for the times. They helped her find employment by reading our mother's ad in the special home "classified" section of the <u>Cleveland Plain Dealer</u>.

To say she was an angel – with a disposition to match – is an elevated understatement!

She helped Mary E. hone skills that profited her the rest of her life.

She taught Mary E. to manage her time, so that one project determined the progress of another – as in putting together Mary's first bicycle. (They saved the crate that it came in to build a bookcase for Mary and Jane's room.)

Keeping and following all instructions – always – was another lesson and why the pedals were properly attached – right and left foot on the right and left side of the bike. (Jane did her own a year later – the pedals fell off – threads destroyed by putting the left on the right and the right on the left.)

Jane gave Betty many challenges. She spent a lot of time finding "wrongs" her world needed to correct – *and right now*. As injustices abound, Betty has quieted many an outburst by introducing Jane to an embroidery hoop! Jane sits quietly – completely engrossed and out of trouble, making beautiful French knots and the chain stitch on squares to create a quilt.

She is 90 now and will finish enough squares any day.

LESSON: WHEN WE COUNT OUR BLESSINGS, WE COUNT BETTY TWICE! (IRISH PROVERB)

Carolyn is a complete contrast to Jane. She is the "Dutch" side of the family, the first to have shiny blond hair and sparkling blue eyes and a true lady-like demeanor. (She once wore white gloves to Euclid Beach Park to ride "the Thriller.")

Betty could relax. Carolyn was never going to steal the neighbor's flowers – that was Mary and Jane. She was never going to get stuck in the drain pipe on the roof – that was Mary E.

She was never going to eat the onions from a gunny sack in the garage – that was Alberta.

Carolyn excels at math and beats our smart Uncle Will at Chinese checkers. He is so impressed, he makes ballet lessons possible. Aunt Carrie sends Carolyn – her namesake – a diamond ring for her 16th birthday.

## LESSON: WHAT'S IN A NAME? A LOT!

Alberta takes care of herself and loves following Betty around to help with chores. Consequently, Alberta thinks for herself, loves classical music (her sisters are "gone" on Frank Sinatra), and is the first to think "marriage" after a blind date at eighteen. (Jane arranged the date and never forgives herself for breaking up "The Sisters.")

The 30s continue, with a new son, but a new challenge takes place – not in the nursery – in the city itself!

Ray T. Miller is mayor of Cleveland. He names Al Sutphin Boxing and Wrestling Commissioner.

The duties include supervising all "weigh-ins" before every match and the inspection of boxing gloves to determine if illegal weights are hidden.

Judge Frank Merrick brings his official O.K. to the process.

Even though past his prime, the name "Johnny Kilbane" is common dinner-table conversation at the Sutphin home.

(By 2014, Cleveland will boast three bronze statues – with weightless gloves – of that feisty "Golden Gloves" favorite.)

Albert and Mary Sutphin's children, meanwhile, have joined Ray Miller's children, both at St. Ann School and at Friday afternoon skating at the famous Elysium at E. 107th and Euclid Avenue, owned by Harvey Humphrey.

In the summer, both families love Mr. Humphrey's other grand endeavor, "Euclid Beach Park," on Lake Erie.

There, everyone can enjoy swimming, a dance hall, a Hall of Mirrors, an arcade for games and skee-ball, and scary rides like "The Thriller."

Taking home taffy candy kisses and popcorn balls are a must (still available in 2015 in local grocery stores).

Back at the Elysium, skating lessons and "open" ice skating to music are practiced until spring.

Suddenly, there is talk of an ice hockey man named Harry "Hap" Holmes. His hockey team, called "the Indians" in the International Hockey League, is competing on Saturday nights at the Elysium. Since seating is limited to 1,000 fans, another 1,000 are turned away.

Al Sutphin is intrigued!

He begins attending all Saturday night home hockey games, and becomes impressed with a very loyal and smitten hockey crowd.

Al and "Hap" Holmes are now close friends, making it possible for Al Sutphin to learn about the love, but also financial trials, of owning a hockey team without a rink big enough to accommodate a big and paying fan base.

"Hap" confides that he has lost his team; the bank has foreclosed.

Al Sutphin buys the team and renames them "The Falcons."

His greatest adventure begins!

How to borrow money?

Clevelanders are not feeling good about the future; joblessness and soup kitchens abound. It is a dark and hurting place. The banks are not loaning money. Al Sutphin soon learns, when the banker stands up behind his desk, the interview is over, and so is the loan.

Re-enter Judge Frank Merrick. His law duties have made it possible for him to form connections all over Ohio. Judge Merrick contacts Al Sutphin. The good Judge suggests that Al Sutphin contact a great industrialist and owner of Union Central Life Insurance, Mr. Charles Sawyer.

When the two men met in Cincinnati, Mr. Sawyer declared, "Albert, I've been watching you. You are a go-getter, a very hard-working young man, with business know-how. I think you can do this."

At Union Central Life Insurance Company in Cincinnati, Albert Sutphin signs on to borrow one million dollars, with Charles Sawyer as the second signee.

Al Sutphin is 39 years old.

Mr. Sawyer did not mention his age.

The terms of the loan: 300 events – not just hockey – must take place in the building, with a paying audience.

Al Sutphin will be booking many attractions, but, just as important, he must learn the pitfalls and successes of building a large enough arena to house 9,950 paying customers.

Albert realizes he must visit every successful arena in the country to learn the logistics of making ice for hockey and ice shows and, within 48 hours, have a trained crew that can set up for a circus or a six-day bike race.

He realizes that he will be talking to engineers, builders, food managers, and box office personnel, and he will be learning about interviewing and hiring hundreds of employees.

Ed Bang, venerable sports editor of the <u>Cleveland News</u>, sent Al Sutphin a right-hand man, Norbert Stein, to see him through the first season, 1937.

Norbert lasted all twelve years of Al Sutphin's Arena presidency, and no one questioned if he could have handled it all without Norbert's newspaper press releases, his people skills, patience, know-how, and personal sacrifice.

After 1949, Norbert became an ink salesman for Braden Sutphin and made a great many friends and homeruns in a whole new ballgame.

Cleveland newspaper and sports writers ignited the interest essential to selling the idea to the general public and to the movers and doers of industry to become investors.

Whitey Lewis, sports editor of the <u>Cleveland Press</u>, was a personal friend and as interested in seeing a hockey and all-event palace in Cleveland as Al Sutphin was.

Al's biggest challenge was meeting the interest payments of $60,000 a year on the $1,000,000 loan.

He accomplished the impossible in just eighteen months through a large group of companies sold on the idea of advertising their products throughout the Arena and renewing every year!

The following are a few who made the Arena possible:

Engle Fetzer Furrier
McDonough Motors
W. A. Jones Optical
Richman Brothers Co.
Cannon Tailoring
Lucioni's Restaurant
Bartunek Brothers

The Northeast Ohio Ford Dealers Association gave thirty Fords away the first year at each home hockey game (1937-1938). The Ford Dealers Association contributed $300 for each car, and the Cleveland Arena donated the matching $300.

The next financial challenge of $500,000 per year to meet operating expenses was to find investors ("Believers") to purchase debenture bonds, which would pay a yearly interest rate.

Where to find these "Believers?"

Everywhere! When Al Sutphin succeeded in getting someone to listen, he was almost impossible to ignore!

The newspapers wrote columns saying that 98% of those approached became investors.

One ideal opportunity to capture friends came from Saturday night parties at Al and Mary Sutphin's new and bigger home on Berkshire Road, just two blocks up and one block over from their former home – still in Cleveland Heights – and one block from Mary's mother, Florence Hoynes.

The "lure" was the opportunity to meet the whole new, young, handsome hockey team members who acted as co-hosts and impressed everyone with their youth, personalities and gracious manners.

The four Sutphin daughters were part of the team. Mary E. – now 12 – was in charge of the bar. She gathered 72 old-fashioned glasses. Jane – 10 – put a drop of bitters on the small sugar cube. Carolyn – 8 – sliced the oranges. Alberta – 6 – readies the maraschino cherries, and our Dad will add the bourbon at "show time" – 7:30 p.m. The seltzer follows, and we hope that the investors do, too!

Meanwhile, the indispensable "Marie" has been creating her Swedish magic in the kitchen. Since noon, with our mother as helper, Marie takes mountains of ingredients, waves a magic wand, and out jump canapés that have the female guests asking for her phone number.

Who can't love a red pimiento and green olive wrapped in bacon, or crab meat on a toasted cheese circle with capers?

From these impressed and worthy guests will emerge six loyal officers, the Executive Board of Cleveland Hockey, Inc., and the Arena Corporation.

Albert Sutphin will be President and First Officer.

These men are leaders on the Cleveland scene in the 1930s.

> Ellis Ryan (Insurance) – First Vice President
> C. F. Lezius (Lezius-Hiles Printing) – Second Vice President
> J. Fred Potts (Legal Counsel) – Secretary
> Timothy J. Conway (Fisher Foods) – Treasurer
> J. A. Gideon (J. C. Hub Printing)
> Don Robertson

Also from the Cleveland scene, the following "Believers" will become Directors of Cleveland Hockey, Inc. and the Arena Corporation:

| | |
|---|---|
| Ellwood Fisher | owner of Fisher Foods |
| Paul Hoynes | Central Electrotype |
| C. E. Sutphin | father, and Central Ohio Paper |
| A. M. Miller | Columbus, Ohio |
| F. W. Danner | Danner Press, Akron, Ohio |
| Frank Conat | |
| G. L. Erikson | Braden Sutphin Ink |
| Lester Grimes | Advertising |

The Christmas of 1936 must have remained etched in the minds of Cleveland industry leaders who had not seen contracts – nor work – for a long time!

Gillmore-Carmichael-Olson Co. are the contractors, and Lavelle Plumbing has a huge contract that reportedly *"made* their Christmas."

Christmas hymns come to mind when jobs, jobs, jobs were created, and there was something to sing about.

Carpenters, electricians, painters, masons, stadium seat manufacturers, costume and athletic equipment creators, ushers, food experts – hundreds found work – and thousands bought tickets!

In all the excitement, a new American Hockey League was born – founded by Al Sutphin and eight other Arena owners with hockey teams in towns all over the Eastern United States: Hershey, Pa., Pittsburgh, Pa., Springfield, Ma., Buffalo, N.Y., Providence, R.I., Indianapolis, In.

The National Hockey League – long famous for the N.Y. Rangers, the Detroit Red Wings, The Chicago Black Hawks, Toronto Maple Leafs, Montreal Canadiens, and Boston Bruins – now had a new kid on the block. And the Cleveland kid had a new name. "The Falcons" had become "The Barons."

Al Sutphin held a "naming contest." There had to be a "slogan" with the name – which would decide the winner. The winning slogan was "Let's follow the aristocrats of hockey." A cartoon-type figure wearing a tall silk hat, a tuxedo and a monocle completed the picture.

Al Sutphin has created an image of hard work and honesty, so much so that when he approached friends and the public – in general – to sell his "dream," 98% of those approached became investors.

His barber, Lou Griffen, took from his cash drawer the only $100 bill he had. In handing it over, he declared, "You know, Al, I think you're going to do this thing."

"Faith built the Arena," columnist Ed McAuley wrote. "Al Sutphin's word was priceless." (As quoted in The Man in the Arena by George Condon)

The ground-breaking ceremony takes place on May 9, 1937, at 3700 Euclid Avenue, formerly part of "Millionaires' Row," and former site of Charles Brush's mansion.

Whitey Lewis, sports editor of the Cleveland Press, holds the mike as Master of Ceremonies. His enthusiastic columns and close personal friendship made him the right man for the "occasion impossible."

There were nine "Believers" (directors) holding silver shovels, festooned with purple ribbons, the first three being:

Al Sutphin, as President, takes the first "dig."

Eleanor Braden follows next – a worthy successor and acting in her husband Jim Braden's memory.

Ernie Sutphin takes his turn as he ponders "financial independence and self-reliance" – his first lessons for his son, Albert.

Just six months later, on November 10, 1937 – the Arena is born!

It takes center stage in a hurting place – Albert and Mary Sutphin's "Home Town."

It is a night for "full court dress," and Clevelanders have packed the nearly 10,000 seats.

It's all here! It all happened! A glowing Ice Follies awaits backstage.

The ice glitters with a checkerboard black and white pattern – a first!

The Sutphin family – Albert and Mary, their five children, Mary E., Jane, Carolyn, Alberta, and five-year-old Jimmy – are introduced, along with Albert's parents, Ernie and Bess Sutphin, and Mary's mother, Florence Hoynes, and Mary's brothers and sister.

Next, the spotlight finds all the Directors and Officers and their beautifully-dressed wives – possibly wearing Engle-Fetzer furs.

A huge bouquet of roses has a life of its own. Mary Sutphin is spotlighted receiving the bouquet. From then on, as the lights brighten and dim, it is thrust into the arms of all the wives of Directors and Officers of the Arena Corporation.

LESSON: A WELL-TRAINED STAFF CAN PASS THEIR FIRST TEST: ONE BOUQUET, SEVENTEEN RECIPIENTS, AND NOT A WILTED PETAL.

Money was tight, and before the evening was over, almost everyone else knew the same glow!

Jane asked her Dad, "Is this the happiest night of your life?" He answered, "I've borrowed one million dollars, I'm scared to death – but don't tell anyone!"

She didn't – until she was 90!

The conductor of the Ice Follies orchestra raises his baton (many Cleveland musicians are included for this extraordinary night), the overture begins, the "dream" now comes to life with music, and the enthusiastic Clevelanders are not disappointed!

The skaters are wearing glittering costumes, the lighting traces their routines, and they are flawless!

As those thousands of excited Clevelanders entered the new Arena that November night, they were greeted by an illuminated banner running the full width of the long lobby, just inside the glass front doors, proclaiming, "THEY HAD CONFIDENCE," which also enshrined the names of every investor – including Albert's barber, who invested his only one-hundred-dollar bill.

There are hundreds of names representing "Believers" from Cleveland and all surrounding areas – Chagrin Falls, Canton, Akron, Niles, Youngstown, Warren, and certainly Cincinnati. This banner remained in place all the days of the Arena's existence.

One man stands front and center above all those who made this extraordinary night possible – James Braden – who had been the very first believer in Al Sutphin! As he recognized "a bright young man" on that streetcar in 1914, he gave Al Sutphin every opportunity to succeed.

He put Albert in charge of running the Braden Ink Company office. He taught him how to make ink, to hone his selling skills with honesty and a hard-work enthusiasm that would capture customers, making them life-long friends!

By 1929, "being The Boss" meant being alone to run the company.

Albert sent "the check" each month to Jim Braden's widow.

The mystery continues. One hundred thirty-five direct descendants will never know how much Albert Sutphin paid for the Braden Ink Company.

At the brand-new, glistening Arena, the sight of nearly 10,000 seats, enhanced by Al Sutphin's love of red, white and blue, was a sight to behold.

*Blue* seats dominated the entire upper half of the interior – $.75 for hockey games.

The *white* seats were half of the lower Arena – at $1.25 for home hockey games.

*Red*, Al Sutphin's favorite color, gave fans a box seat on the ice for $2.50.

A number of "special" guests might find themselves in the Press Box – way up near the ceiling, if the Press had a night off – and not a home hockey game to report.

Albert's red tie could be spotted in the family red box seats, in the Press Box, in the Pilsner Cellar restaurant, at a food stand, or while he was shaking hands with people as happy as he was that it had all happened.

Of course, they didn't owe one million dollars!

His ties – all bright red – always were his trademark cravats. Many fans thought that the one they saw was the only one he had, and felt sorry for him! Actually, he bought them a gross at a time.

Advertisers were featured in the hockey program and around the Arena.

Richman Brothers' clock couldn't be missed. It hung from the ceiling squarely in the center of the Arena, with sides facing North, East, South, and West, with the scores for all to see.

Ellis Ryan and his insurance company became a tenant.

Dick Krozen opened a new, much-larger sporting goods store – occupying one-half of the entire front lobby of the Arena.

Dick Krozen and Al Sutphin became very popular comics on the dinner circuit with their pitch to lure investors into the coming Arena – Dick had his punch line: "Al Sutphin has built his Arena directly behind my new sporting goods store!"

Imagine having available to fans: athletic jerseys, sweat pants, gloves, goggles, jackets, socks, shoes, hockey sticks, pucks, shin guards, helmets – all for sale right in the Arena – ice skates, too!

And just in case of emergency, Dr. Lust and Dr. Begg moved their surgical office to the handy second floor.

LESSON: LOCATION, LOCATION, LOCATION.

In the years that Al Sutphin travelled to book those 300 events – to satisfy the terms of the loan – he met skaters, actors, comics, swimmers, and dancers just starting out and looking for a break. When the cost of a hotel room was prohibitive, they stayed at the Sutphin's home – just 22 minutes from the Arena.

Question: How many elementary school children come home for lunch and find a midget living with them?

Answer: All the lucky ones!

Enter Count Neihauser! He was a perfectly groomed midget who was about to appear at the Arena for a week, performing as a magic act.

Enter our two-year-old brother, Cal. When the Count and Cal were introduced, and stood facing one another, both were three feet tall. The Count was wearing a tuxedo, a large diamond ring, and was smoking a cigar. Cal was wearing his best velvet romper suit covering his fresh diaper.

Rather than greet our guest, Cal began blinking, blinking, blinking – he couldn't stop blinking. He was hurried off to have dinner upstairs.

The Count smoothly followed the rest of the family into the dining room. He entertained us all with fascinating tales of life on the road in Nazi Germany – escaping police who demanded identification papers his manager couldn't produce. All over Europe, very serious changes were taking place.

Our next memorable houseguest was a complete change.

Hazel Franklin travelled with her affable and very proper mother, Peggy Franklin.

Mary E. moved to the third floor, and our guests enjoyed her room with a view of the backyard.

Hazel Franklin was billed as England's "12-year-old skating sensation – London-born." They had signed a contract for a one-week performance – with other skating acts.

Hazel stole the show!

That week, our parents drove Hazel and her mother to the Arena, and all of us attended every performance, not getting to bed before 11:30 p.m. – school night or not!

We followed Hazel's career all the way to her performances with the Ice Follies.

We became such good friends that Hazel felt comfortable confiding in us that when she skated as the "twelve-year-old sensation," she was almost fifteen!

LESSON: JUDGING A BOOK BY ITS COVER ISN'T ALL BAD.

Here comes Sonja Henie!

She skated into our lives a whole different kind of ice ballerina. Her routines included a tall, handsome Michael Kirby – gold medal 1942

Canadian champion, and a celebrity in his own right. But it was hard to notice *him*!

Sonja had an entourage of publicity people, maids, hairdressers, make-up people, and account managers. The accountants meant that business was booming at Sonja's bank.

By the time Sonja had negotiated her contracts, the Arena barely made expenses. Her first demand was a beautiful backstage dressing room, as never seen before.

The Arena engaged a Miss Cantillon. With incredible skill, Miss Cantillon created a pink velvet tent, featuring mirrored walls, special lighting, a marble dressing table, and a bathroom with a shower. We four little Sutphin girls were struck dumb at the sight.

Sonja said, "It lacked good taste."

Al Sutphin was so frustrated that he called Art Wirtz, owner and manager of the Chicago Stadium, where Sonja had performed before coming to Cleveland. "How do you handle her?!" Sutphin asked.

"That's easy," declared Mr. Wirtz, "I just lock up her mink coat and tell her when she acts like a lady, I'll return it!"

She raved about her admiration for Mr. Wirtz and always gave him any booking date he requested – a very big show business advantage – every arena wants New Year's Eve.

We four little Sutphin skaters begged to meet Sonja.

Our mother already had drawn attention to the way she held her beautiful hands while performing.

Our audience was arranged for the foyer of her penthouse at the Park Lane Villa at E. 107th, overlooking the Art Museum park. She picked a school day. We skipped afternoon classes.

Our appointment was scheduled for 2:30 p.m. At 5:30 p.m., she appeared, wrapped in a magnificent mink coat (fresh from Chicago lock-up, perhaps).

We were mesmerized! She was gorgeous!

Thankfully, we had made a scrapbook of all her skating shows and movies from newspapers and movie magazine articles. The stories all claimed that she and Tyrone Power were "an item." We soon vouched for that!

Sonja spent 20 of our allotted 25 minutes mesmerized by every picture or article in our scrapbook of the two of them – Tyrone's eyes ablaze, Sonja wearing her big, happy smile – arms entwined!

Seeing Sonja into her limo and rushing home to fill pages in our diaries, we say hello to the 30s-plus and more adventures.

The summers of 1932, 1933, and 1934 were spent at "Shore Acres," a cottage retreat on Lake Erie at the foot of E. 185th Street. (Euclid General Hospital stands there today.)

It had seen better days. The lingering Depression had turned summer guests into struggling permanent residents.

"Smitty" – our sea-side neighbor – was a handyman, advisor, good Dad to two sons, and knew everything about lake-side living.

Ruby Delaney's boat-shaped structure was called her "last hurrah." She was holding on in a dilapidated, unpainted, old cabin cruiser that was completely falling apart. Her welcoming smile and her home-grown kohlrabi – sold from her doorstep – made us love to visit her.

We watched her as she handled "farming" from her bib-apron pockets filled with trowels and rusty scissors.

Those three summers became an awakening – in every way – for four little sisters and a brand-new baby brother, one month old.

We learned to make our own way among strangers – in a strange, watery world dominated by wind and sun, clouds and sky – even earth that can feed us.

We learn new chores!

We meet a challenge of new ways to spend our days – discovering new places, new people – even new Mom and Dad.

Our mother doesn't go in the water, but she wears something called "beach pajamas" – with very long, wide, flowing legs that female guests want to copy.

Dad's "itchy" black wool one-piece bathing suit was "all the rage" for men.

He made our day complete! When he returned each late afternoon from Braden Sutphin Ink downtown, we all ran for our rubber bathing suits.

Dad was our swimming instructor – and we learned fast!

His training methods were unorthodox and no-nonsense.

He threw us into knee-deep water, shouting "paddle hard!" all the while keeping eyes alert and a close watch on Alberta, who was only four.

We were soon "mermaids" – whatever they were!

Meanwhile, we learned about boy babies. Jimmy doesn't look like us at all. He sleeps a lot and is so small that we cannot play with him. He seems to be in great need of his wonderful nurse, Betty Cook, who plainly loves him. We did, too, when he finally smiled.

### LESSON: BOYS NEED LOTS OF ATTENTION – EVEN IF THEY AREN'T MUCH FUN!

We had new chores!

Sweeping sand out of the house was really a pain – but the challenge of growing vegetables in a big garden was very new and very enlightening.

Our mother wisely let us choose seed packets containing our own favorite vegetables.

Preparing the site, turning the soil over – to make rows – is daunting.

But the eating – that is miraculous.

Jane's peas and carrots appear often.

Carolyn's beets – her only favorite – and green beans were a staple.

Alberta's lettuce and tomatoes held daily sway.

Mary E. is mentioned last because she planted a dessert – watermelon – vines and all rule the day.

### LESSON: HAPPILY WE ARE SAVING OUR FAMILY AND NEIGHBOR FROM STARVATION. NICE GOING!

As Mary E.'s vines wandered, so did Mary E. – looking for a new challenge.

For her ninth and belated birthday, she has requested a load of lumber.

Our Dad was intrigued! Girls now amaze him!

Smitty taught Mary E. what she wanted to know – how to build a boat!

Dampening lumber and changing its shape – held in a vise – was tricky business.

When – at long last – tar paper was applied to the bottom, the "Queen Mary" set sail.

Thirty feet off shore, the "Queen Mary" floundered.

Undaunted, the lumber was saved, and Mary E. set about building her three sisters a Play House.

The Play House was tall enough to walk around in upright. An orange crate allowed a window view of Lake Erie, and the tar paper kept the rain from soaking inside.

The sisters played every day in their own house – even their dolls loved it. Mary E. moved on!

She began taking ice-cold soda pop to all the neighbors – after Smitty arranged for a delivery guy to supply her. At five cents a pop – and many hot summer days – business was booming!

Meanwhile, under a tarp in the garage, was something sternly identified as *"Don't touch!"*

Every week-end, the family had important guests – our Dad's favorite ink-business friends from Cleveland, Akron and Canton.

When the pop ran out – one very hot day – Mary *touched!*

It was the bootlegged beer that Dad had arranged for this week-end's guests.

Mary felt noble! Instead of five cents, she charged *ten cents*, and the word spread. Soon, lines were forming, and the rush was on!

Our Dad gave us our first glimpse into cardiac arrest.

A fast call to the closest bootlegger – who never sleeps – saved the week-end.

What saved *us*? We were very carefully engaged in setting the dinner table – just right – that week-end.

The sisters were well practiced at putting the "joke" forks around – the ones with the tines that bend when used. There were also the etched water glasses that spill down everyone's front and – the show-stopper – the serving dishes that explode when raised to pass around the table.

From a paint can in the garage, Mary E. and Jane had been smoking Lucky Strikes most of the summer. Late one summer evening, at dinner time, our Mother and Dad announced a new ritual – "Mary E. and Jane will have a cigarette before dinner this evening."

The girls were dumbfounded – but there was no backing out.

They took a few puffs, but for the first time – with everyone watching – they were dizzy and sick. As they stumbled upstairs – without dinner – the laughter echoed throughout the house.

They always wondered who found those Lucky Strikes in the paint can in that infamous garage.

At the entrance to Shore Acres in the early 1930s stood an architectural wonder! A T.B. Sanitarium in the shape of a giant silver "Golf Ball" – every little divot represented a window where patients were exposed to the sunlight's "magical cure."

When the county opened Sunny Acres on Warrensville Center Road, all the patients were relocated there.

In our last summer – 1934 – our new neighbor at the entrance was Herman Pirchner's Alpine Village, where the Sutphin family held a farewell to their Lake Erie odyssey.

At the table were Smitty and his boys and Ruby Delaney, wearing her exotic best turban in a shade of flaming orange.

This is no longer the same Sutphin family.

These are children who are three years older and decades wiser! The baby, Jimmy, laughs a lot, walks and runs, and can tell you he's now seen an alligator come out of its shell, which is now in a cage at Smitty's place.

Back in town, the Sutphin girls were not permitted to cross Derbyshire Road in Cleveland Heights, because it was a speedway for drivers avoiding Euclid Heights Boulevard traffic.

They had spent three healthy summers roaming 50 sparsely settled acres of woods and beach and parkland.

They had grown their own food and always shared with their neighbors.

They had proven to themselves that the earth provides everything needed to be alive and thrive.

They will return home able to protect themselves – they are pugilists now, taught by Smitty's weekly boxing lessons.

Just as important, they find themselves as people who have physically faced every possible condition of surf, wind and water – and survived!

Their second summer, in 1933, they endured a serious tornado while their Mother was out and late to return – in her Model A Ford.

All electricity was out. Torrential rain, heavy flooding, downed trees, and wind were in charge.

Just seeing the turmoil taking place on Lake Erie was enough to make them scared to death.

But "calm" prevailed for 1934 – the Sutphin family's final summer on beautiful, *clean* Lake Erie! It was a lifetime of learning moments to be reflected upon day by day at home.

We finalize the 30s with an outstanding and life-altering event. Our parents astound us with a new baby brother, Albert Carleton, seven years after Jimmy.

It is 1939! We have noticed nothing about our mother to tip us off that big changes are occurring!

It is the week of their 17$^{th}$ wedding anniversary, and they are away somewhere. We imagine a resort for belated honeymooners. Little do we realize that the honeymoon is long over! They are at St. Ann Maternity Hospital on Woodland Avenue in downtown Cleveland, and we will be preparing a blue and white nursery. Soon, brother Jimmy will have a roommate.

Jane is thrilled! Her friends are noticing boys, but Jane – at fourteen – is still playing with dolls. Now, she has a real baby doll. She insists on being a second mother, and puts Cal on her top priority list!

Cal is so cute!

The sisters show no restraint:

> *Mary E.* buys all of his clothes!
> *Jane* gives him his bottles and, finally, solids.
> *Carolyn* introduces him to books by reading to him.
> *Alberta* plays classical music for him.
> *Jimmy* is his pal in sports.

Cal – now, unfairly spoiled – wants his own way. He is also seriously afflicted with asthma, and sees a fine specialist, Dr. Horesh.

Cal grows up fast!

As our parents are in Ft. Myers for the winter, Jimmy and Cal go to school there.

In Cal's day, he plays serious baseball for Ft. Myers High School, and he and his Dad join forces for all high school away games – supplying some of the transportation.

As our parents return to Cleveland in May each year, Cal remains in Ft. Myers with sister Alberta and husband Ray Stoney and their now-six children.

They are auxiliary parents for Cal through some of his high school years.

Our big family secret is this:

The four sisters – at home – have been left in the care of a carefully selected housekeeper, from a very select agency, called Sar Louis.

They will be amazed to discover that they are really "home alone," as Mrs. X, the housekeeper, has a drinking problem – and passes out by 7:00 p.m.!

Since they are the best-brought-up and trustworthy girls of Catholic school education and religion – and tough Dutch rules and regulations – they pray for Mrs. X, do their homework, keep the house clean, do the dishes, and go to the movies every night!

There never is a reason to report this! – until years later, when reminiscing with their mother, who declared, "You girls were not chaperoned!"

She is left shell-shocked!

But we know that Mary E. was the best leader and caregiver, who would never have allowed us the opportunity to dishonor our family name!

**LESSON: ALL IS WELL THAT WORKS WELL IN SECRET.**

Al Sutphin may have believed in higher education, but the 40s find his children very involved in Arena affairs. Enjoy!

# CHAPTER III

# THE 1940S

The longer Al Sutphin runs the Arena, the more a promoter he becomes! – And the more those growing daughters (now in their late teens and early 20s) will be called upon to prove themselves in business and in some of that promoting!

For Albert, the job of finding big audiences is a challenge that brings focus on the towns and small cities surrounding the Cleveland area. They include Canton, Warren, Niles, and Youngstown.

One 1940s inspiration was to promote the opening of the Arena winter season – in September – with a big publicity stunt.

The Ice Capades that year was featuring the Disney classic, Snow White and the Seven Dwarfs.

Al Sutphin arranged for Ellen Robertson, Publicity Director, to train daughter, Jane, and include her in making the rounds to four towns and small cities surrounding Cleveland. Jane and Ellen will spend one week on the road introducing themselves to the Entertainment Editors of the <u>Niles Daily Times</u>, the Canton <u>Repository</u>, the Warren <u>Tribune Chronicle</u>, and the Youngstown <u>Vindicator</u>.

Their objective is attracting the attention, through the newspapers, of an extraordinary event coming to their towns – dates to be decided – and announced to their respective readers.

In August, a 30-foot-long Ice Capades float will arrive at noon – on their town squares!

"Snow White" will man a loudspeaker and announce the dates of the Ice Capades event at the Cleveland Arena and ticket prices. Music will be playing! She will then send skyward hundreds of balloons, some with two free tickets attached (causing people to roam the countryside in pursuit).

Noon is the time selected to attract the "lunch hour" crowd from stores and businesses.

Parked next to the float will be a "traveling box office" – from the Arena – with Nate Dolan in charge. He sells tickets while "Snow White" mans the helium machine to send up the balloons.

The box office returned each day to Cleveland as the float traveled town to town, and "Snow White" stayed in a motel.

When our Dad announced to our Mother that Jane, who looked just like Snow White, would drive the float and perform all duties for a week on the road, our Mother finally decided it was time to have him committed.

## LESSON: AS THE ROSARY COMES OUT, "OKAY" OUTCOMES PREVAIL!

On the night before the Canton event, Jane parks the float in *North* Canton on the street of a dear friend from her Laurel School days. She is Lillian Brendel, now Somers. She and Deke have two sons so far – two more later.

The fun begins!

On the street, the float is surrounded by every neighbor – and their kids – from blocks around!

Jane announces that there will be "Big Events" the next day in downtown *Canton* itself, and gets everyone excited. Apparently, the Repository did not extend so much to *North* Canton.

Jane sleeps on the float, has breakfast with the Somers family, and heads for noon on Canton's city square!

The neighborhood never forgot the night "Snow White" and the Seven Dwarfs slept on their street.

She doesn't see Lil again until the Somerses move to Fairmount Boulevard in Cleveland Heights, and they become godparents for each other's children.

As earlier reported, when Al Sutphin took $1.00 a year for his Arena salary, he had still another idea in mind.

Albert saw the hockey program as a great vehicle for income.

The challenge became his!

He considered the Program a very personal endeavor.

For an entire summer – each year from 1937 to 1949 – he found a way and the time to make a personal call on each of his loyal and friendly advertisers.

He wore his uniform drip-dry blue suit, his white shirt, and his very red tie for all twelve years.

It was reported that some people felt sorry for Al Sutphin – with only *one* red tie!

One advertiser asked his receptionist, "Is my next appointment wearing a very red tie?" When she answered, "Yes," her Boss said, "That's Al Sutphin – send him in."

There were thirty home games for the AHL Cleveland Barons. The Arena program soon announced "lucky numbers" on many of the advertisers' company ads. They were giving away their companies' products at every home game to a lucky winner who found that he had the "lucky number" in his program.

Within a year or two, the hockey program grew to ninety-eight 8 ½" by 11" pages.

The hockey officials complained, "If a fan resents a 'call' I make, being hit by that program could kill me."

Al had another idea in mind. It involved his youngest daughter, Alberta. Her role was vital, because she performed a ten-minute skating routine, and then delivered the much-awaited certificate, awarding the lucky winner ownership of a gift prize.

It was difficult for Al Sutphin to run out of daughters or ideas.

In the later 1940s, daughter Mary E. was involved – daily – in the two-for-one ticket sales, both selling and then delivering large orders of "event" tickets.

Including the new kid on the block professional basketball, she sold to the local war plants – Jack & Heintz, Thompson Products, and Cadillac Tank Plant.

Two tickets for the price of one created sold-out opening nights.

The war plants bought hundreds of tickets – as gifts – for their hard-working, war-weary employees.

Mary loved her job!

Al Sutphin then created a Friday night extravaganza. A $.50 student ticket or a two-for-one entitled the ticket holder to a double-header basketball evening.

To build interest on both sides of town – East and West – John Carroll University would play Baldwin Wallace every Friday night in the first match. Following that were scheduled two of the best national college teams in the country – the University of Kentucky and Holy Cross come to mind.

Students and fans then stayed for an hour of dancing to a live Cleveland popular orchestra.

While helping out, one event stands alone!

Mary and Jane are assigned Cloak Room duty on a basketball night – with dancing afterward.

The Cloak Room is a long, narrow passageway, directly off the basketball floor, offering easy access to all fans – especially students staying for dancing.

As Mary E. accepts coats and gives out numbered tickets, Jane hangs the coats and sends them to the rear on a wire.

As the evening extends into hours, Mary asks Jane if she smells something burning.

As the very last dancing couple claim their coats, the young student cries out, "My coat is on fire!"

Mary E. assesses the damage. The right shoulder of the student's brown muskrat fur coat has been resting for six hours against a 250-watt bulb!

Mary E. – her usual unflappable self – reassures the young lady that everything will be taken care of at once.

Jane, meanwhile, is pretending she isn't there.

Mary notifies our loyal and trusty advertiser, Engel-Fetzer Furrier, who picks up the coat – at the student's home – and returns it within three days *better* than new. The new shoulder pelt is – by far – the best quality of all the pelts in the coat.

Mary E. rates right up there that evening with Alberta missing the sled and having to skate out and hop on – with thousands of Baron hockey fans laughing hilariously!

Jane's publicity job was more glamorous, with more personal contacts to handle!

She introduced herself to the latest stars – Donna Atwood with the Ice Capades, the Scotvold twins, Joanne and Joyce, with Ice Follies, and the perennial favorites, the Old Smoothies.

Jane would arrange interviews with the Entertainment Editors of all three Cleveland newspapers – the <u>Plain Dealer</u>, the <u>Press</u>, and the <u>News</u>.

She would arrive at the star's hotel – an hour before the interview – to bone up on the interview story.

Sometimes, the star wasn't ready – or barely awake.

Then, a transformation would take place – a half-awake young performer became a coifed, glamorously made-up, figure-skating star – in twenty minutes.

The Scotvold twins were favorites. Their story was unique. They were "mirror" twins, born in one sac, facing one another. One was right-handed, the other left. Their hair rotated, one clockwise, the other, counter-clockwise.

Their Dad, Evy Scotvold, Sr., had been a Cleveland Falcon hockey player from Minneapolis during the years of 1936 and 1937. Our young brother, Jimmy, had a crush on *both* twins – claiming he could always tell them apart.

Evy Scotvold, Jr., and his wife, Mary, became figure skating coaches for Olympic hopefuls Nancy Kerrigan and Paul Wylie. (Jane accompanied the Scotvold family to the Nationals in Detroit in 1994 when Tonya Harding and Nancy Kerrigan had their altercation.)

Meanwhile, the Ice Shows sell out and become – after hockey – the Arena's most popular events.

Enter Mary Frances Ackerman – who was hired by John Harris of the Ice Capades fame.

She was a Drama major and aspired to be a movie star.

She agreed to be "Advance Girl" just long enough for the Ice Capades to reach Los Angeles for their long summer break.

An "Advance Girl" travels two weeks ahead of the opening night performance. She contacts the entertainment editors of all the local newspapers and "feeds" them stories to be used as publicity just days before the opening night event. An advance person never stays around for an "opening night," as they are long gone to the next town – always two weeks ahead of the next show.

The skaters rehearsed the *new* show every day – the one that would go on the road in the fall.

Every evening, the "old" show would play to paying audiences for revenue to take a new show on the road.

John Harris and his entourage had rented Glenda Farrell's beautiful Spanish mansion for the summer. It was famous for its tiled bridge stretching across the pool.

Glenda Farrell had become famous for creating a very popular sleuth-type character in a series where she starred as "Torchy Blane."

Albert and Mary Sutphin were making final arrangements for their annual visit to Ice Capades summer headquarters in L.A.

This year was special! Jane had been included – for a Laurel School graduation gift.

## LESSON: FAMILIES ARE ALLOWED TO TIRE OF "CALIFORNIA HERE I COME" SUNG BY JANE – OFF-KEY AND LOUDLY.

When the Super Chief delivers the Sutphin family to L.A. airport, John Harris has sent a car!

The sight of a real Hollywood movie star's home is mind-boggling to Jane. Meeting her gorgeous roommate is even more so!

Mary Frances is 23 years old, and is very welcoming to her new roommate – 18-year-old Jane Sutphin – out of high school for two weeks, now.

As Jane wakens in a huge pink room, Mary Frances is sweeping her hair into a French knot.

It is June 22 – time for that screen test she has dreamed of all her life!

As Jane says, "Break a leg," Mary Frances leaves with a wisp of a Hattie Carnegie flower hat above the French knot, and her Schiaparelli black suit – size four – is fitting perfectly. Jane prays she makes it.

Jane will know, personally, a movie star – if all prayers are answered!

Later that night, John Harris, his son, John, Jr. (12 years old), and Jane and her parents pay rapt attention as Mary Frances tells her saga of a film star hopeful at Paramount pictures.

Her co-star was Fred McMurray, who offered to do a scene from his latest film, "Double Indemnity."

She admitted to being nervous because most of her experience at Carnegie Mellon had been on the stage – not in film.

As it turned out, the cherries jubilee dessert at Romanoff's that June night was a bigger hit than Mary Frances' film debut.

Happily for Jane, Mary Frances continues as Ice Capades "Advance Girl," and they connect regularly.

Jane finishes Western Reserve University, Flora Stone Mather College, in the class of '47, and continues to do publicity and promotion for the Arena.

Mary Frances is soon "taken off the market."

Dear friends, Franny and Frank Gibbons (sportswriter for the Cleveland Press) have introduced her to Bill Veeck.

It is a *take*!

Mary Frances has six little Veecks and is here for Cleveland's greatest sport year, 1948. Veeck's Indians win the World Series, the Cleveland Browns win the All-American Football League Championship – a triumph for Paul Brown – and the Cleveland Barons win the Calder Cup.

Hurrah for the red, white, and blue Arena and our Dad – the Champ!

Now, back to 1943 and our farewell to John Harris and Mary Frances in Los Angeles.

On our last day, John Harris arranges a Hollywood studio tour.

He introduces Jane to Harold Lloyd, her all-time favorite comedian – ever – and she takes home an 8 x 10 glossy of Roy Rogers – with his guitar – and all three Sutphins are having a wonderful time!

On to San Francisco, at Ice Follies headquarters, our fantastic reunion with Eddie and Roy Shipstad and Oscar Johnson takes place. Six years earlier, they "opened" the Cleveland Arena with the most beautiful ice show any of us had ever seen – on a magic night of dreams come true!

Now, we see a rehearsal of the "new show," and realize that it will be at the Arena in March 1944, and we will have had a "preview."

Roy Shipstad and beautiful Bess Ehrhardt are married now and still the romantic stars they always were.

Eddie Shipstad and Oscar Johnson are still doing their comic routine to the same audience enthusiasm we remember on opening night at the Arena in 1937.

Boarding another Sleeper means that this leg of our great odyssey will be spent in another country – Canada!

Oh, Canada!

The second half will bring the glory and majesty of the Canadian Rockies into view – and make it impossible to forget!

We will cross Southern Canada from the magnificent Butchart Gardens, and take tea at the Queen Victoria Hotel. On to Vancouver Island, British Columbia, and Jane's favorite – Lake Louise and Banff – on the Southern Pacific Railroad in a compartment with all three of us – for ten days.

By the time we reach Toronto, Ontario, Jane will have made up for all the years she missed our Dad, who had labored under too much pressure and responsibility to be around home.

We have had a glorious time! All three of us are resilient travelers – in one compartment – no greater test – and we like one another still and forever.

Not another sight – anywhere – has ever had the impact of Lake Louise!

For Jane – with a terrible war raging for both Canadians and Americans – never to be forgotten will be the perfection of Mother Nature and the serenity found at Lake Louise on a perfect June day in 1943.

We reach Calgary, Alberta, in time to attend the annual "Stampede," the "greatest *cowboy* show on earth."

This year, a "Mistress of Ceremonies," is the famous fan-dancer and strip-tease artist, Sally Rand, who doesn't disappoint anyone. She can be seen from any seat in the stadium. We're talking about more white leather than could keep ten cows alive.

She is wearing white leather boots to the tip of her white leather skirt, which sets off her white leather jacket. The white leather Stetson cowboy hat is truly the "crowning" feature – except for Sally Rand herself!

She is even more ostentatious than the outfit. She exudes glamour, waving to the spectators, and leaving no doubt that her fame is well earned!

Now begins our one-night stands!

The week will find us in new prairie towns from Medicine Hat, Alberta, to Moose Jaw and Saskatoon, Saskatchewan. We certainly couldn't leave out Winnipeg, Manitoba.

Back in Regina, Alberta, we had a wonderful reunion with Royal Canadian Air Force member, Jim Cook, son of Bill Cook, the Cleveland Barons' first coach and famous New York Ranger player.

By 1943, we will have spent three summers on the Cooks' dairy farm in Kingston, Ontario, on the St. Lawrence River.

Bill Cook, his brother Bun Cook, and Frankie Boucher were the New York Rangers' "most notorious line" in the National Hockey League.

Our visit with Bill Cook's oldest son, Jim, was a huge treat! Back on the dairy farm – before the war in 1940 – Jim and his brothers took the Sutphin girls dancing at a local roadhouse, The Silver Slippers, on Saturday nights.

This "road trip" has a mission! Our Dad is checking in with his hockey scouts to find promising hopefuls to add to the Cleveland Barons' roster – about to be coached by Bun Cook, Bill's brother.

Third brother, Alex Cook, is a "forward" for the Barons.

The Cook "combine" is not surprising.

There is a Cook family legend – the Cook family lived way off in the prairies of Manitoba – nearest neighbor two miles away. During those endless winters with five hockey-playing sons – too cold to skate outside – Mother Cook opened the doors of the large kitchen, watered the floor, made ice, and the Cook boys practiced their "net shots."

With recommendations from the hockey scouts, the young – promising – players would find themselves in Cleveland, Ohio, in the fall, practicing with the Barons.

One season, seven "hopefuls" were housed on the Sutphin family third floor! Two made the squad, but the Sutphin sisters were rooting for all seven.

In early 1940, Bill Cook, the Barons' first coach, had agreed to having the Sutphin family lease a house directly on the St. Lawrence River with a second "cottage" nearby – on an unused part of Cook's dairy farm.

Our Dad was mesmerized with the natural beauty of life on the River and the pine forest surrounding both "cottages."

When Bill Cook explained that his dairy farm would never leave time for swimming and fishing, he was happy to have six young Sutphin children be friends and pal around with his three boys and the light of his life, daughter Billie Marie.

Bill's wife, Clare, became great friends with Mary Sutphin, where friendship extended into winters in Cleveland for the Barons' hockey season.

The cottages needed a picture window, bathrooms, electricity, a platform overlooking the St. Lawrence River's new dock, and a boat.

Bun Cook's mother-in-law, Mrs. Rheume, became our cook, laundress, cleaning person and dearest friend.

Her meals were legendary. Homemade peach ice cream, buns to die for, raspberry shortcake (with berries picked by us), coconut macaroons, steak, and incredible northern pike, smallmouth bass and perch – dinner freshly caught every day by a never-ending parade of guests – printers, friends, Hoyneses, those eleven Conway boys, and Cleveland's many hockey sports writers who found Black Horse Ale and fishing a form of Heaven to be practiced every day!

Mary E. – old enough to drive – was in charge of procurement: bait, ale, groceries, ice, ale, and more Black Horse Ale, and then some Black Horse Ale.

Everybody did everything. Jane was assigned laundry duty with Mrs. Rheume. Mondays and Thursdays, they did 100 towels. Each of those days, Mrs. Rheume washed, and Jane rinsed and hung them up to dry on a wire wheel.

Carolyn and Alberta set tables on a big screened porch overlooking the St. Lawrence River.

We all served and cleared and dried and put away the dishes. Mrs. Rheume washed and cooked.

And Jimmy, now eight (our first year), was taught by Jim Cook how to clean the fish – which had to be done as soon as the fishermen returned at 8 p.m. If fish was on the menu the next day, Jimmy was still cleaning late at night.

As Jimmy grew older, he helped the Cooks with the hay harvest in August – as did all the surrounding neighbors.

We were lucky enough to have Billie Marie fall in love with Jimmy Hoynes – our mother's nephew and our first cousin. They, with their five children, lived near us in Cleveland. Paul Hoynes, long-time Cleveland Indians baseball writer, is their oldest son.

We all loved everything! Swimming every day, pushing the Conway boys – fully dressed – into the icy St. Lawrence.

We also went dancing Saturday nights with the Cook boys at the famous roadhouse down King's Highway II (the main road between Toronto and Montreal).

Three events place our Kingston, Ontario, years in time and place!

The times were World War II, the place was Kingston's Fort Henry – a German prisoner of war camp, four miles south of our "cottage."

Ft. Henry had been the main defense against all enemies since the 17th century.

Directly across the St. Lawrence River – on the American side – was Wolf Island, New York.

As we returned for our second summer – 1941 – Canada was now engaged with Great Britain against Germany and were already receiving prisoners of war.

Fort Henry was no longer a tourist attraction as an historical museum. It was a working prison and, as such, the German war officers considered it their duty to try to escape. Escape meant finding a boat along the civilian waterfront and reaching Wolf Island, where America was not at war – yet.

Every few weeks, the radio would announce another escape from Ft. Henry and another boat stolen from our neighbors on the waterfront.

We worried, but being four miles up the river seemed fairly safe. As it turned out, it wasn't, for us – and five different neighbors lost boats overnight that summer. We lost our Chris Craft!

By our third summer – 1942 – we were engaged in World War II, and thirty prisoners escaped that year. Because they didn't speak English, they were all apprehended on the American side – but they had migrated all over our country.

Our sister, Alberta, reported that the last one to be found was found in California.

Our second adventure involved a promise gone wrong.

Our Dad had promised Jane that if she brought all her grades at Laurel School up to A's, he would allow her to get a driver's license before going to Kingston for the summer of 1942.

Waiting in Kingston was a rare treasure – a car – a 1938 Ford convertible.

Cars were almost impossible to find, as all manufacturers of cars were limited to war vehicles – tanks, jeeps, and staff cars only.

How Bill Cook managed that priceless acquisition we never found out.

Back in Cleveland, when grades were released at the end of school in 1942, Jane had all A's!

This was so impossible a feat, her Dad refused to carry through on his promise. No license – no way!

Jane, totally outraged, went to her mother!

Jane convinced her mother that Dad's promise was a matter of honor.

Mother agreed! (Mothers are so good at this!)

Jane arrived in Kingston with a brand-new driver's license.

It was an "unbreakable rule" that did Jane in!

That priceless car had one flaw! The brakes were fine. The *emergency* brake – not so great.

Therefore, anyone parking in the driveway – 100 feet above the St. Lawrence River – had to place the front bumper against one of the hundreds of pine trees.

It was "barbeque night" – a huge feast outside, on the river at the Sutphin cottage. All the Bill and Bun Cook families were there!

Billie Marie Cook and Jane had been together all evening. Knowing that Jane had a license, Billie asked her to give her a ride home.

The Cook house (Greystone Manor) and farm were up the hill – about a quarter of a mile away.

Jane happily complied. She returned about 11 p.m. It was so dark that Jane thought she had parked against a tall pine tree.

Wrong!

Jane entered the cottage – unseen. As the party-goers watched, the car moved ever so slowly, past one tall pine after another, until it reached the edge of the cliff.

It plunged 100 feet and landed upside down in the river.

Bill Cook and Al Sutphin had seen their daughters get in the car. They did not see them get out. Both Dads plunged over the cliff and began searching the upside-down car for their daughters.

Our mother rushed into the cottage to see if Jane was there!

Fortunately, Jane was able to explain that Billie Marie was at home.

Both fathers had returned from searching the waters. They were cut and bruised. Bill Cook had lost his wallet containing his visa to coach in the U.S., all important cards, and his ready cash.

Our Dad – when he found Jane – shouted, "And you had to drive!"

"Tomorrow, you will sit looking at the crew pulling the car from the river – without food – until it is finished."

Who felt like eating? Not Jane!

It took ten hours of watching and ten years of telling the story!

On a much lighter note, we take a glimpse at our third adventure illustrating life on the river: the practical jokes that ruled the days of fun and games.

Bill Tobin and his wife, Barney, and their daughter, Elaine, never missed a summer!

Bill Tobin was Irish – all the way!

He was "major domo" in Chicago, running the NHL Black Hawks and managing everything that happened at the Chicago Stadium – a huge job!

Everybody loved Barney and Elaine – and gave Mr. Tobin a wide berth.

His first summer, we children didn't know him or his wild Irish humor at all!

Since we treated all guests as royalty, we Sutphins were all standing at attention in the driveway when they arrived!

A short, wise-guy type – with a wicked grin – jumped out of the car and yelled at my not-very-big eight-year-old brother, Jimmy, "Bell boy, get my bags and take them upstairs to my room!"

Jimmy struggled – mightily – up the long outside staircase, pausing often with the weight of the Tobin suitcase.

Bill Tobin waited patiently and then hollered, "Not *that* one – *this* one down here!"

Jimmy struggled all the way downstairs again.

It was soon discovered that Mr. Tobin had filled the suitcase with bricks.

Over the years, Al Sutphin and Bill Tobin spent endless hours of careful planning – to get even!

It started with Elaine Tobin wanting a pony for her tenth birthday! Her father said, "No pony!"

They lived in the high-end suburb of Hinsdale, Illinois.

"No ponies, no grooms, no boarding fees. No! No! No!"

On Elaine's tenth birthday, a live pony was delivered to the Tobin residence, and Mr. Tobin knew immediately that Al Sutphin was to blame.

The pony was named Rosebud, because it ate all of Barney's prized roses.

Bill Tobin got even!

He saved all of Rosebud's droppings for a month, and then mailed them to Al Sutphin in a very large box.

Al Sutphin got even!

When Bill Tobin – by accident – left his golf clubs in Kingston that summer, Al Sutphin was ready!

He removed all clubs, filled the bottom of the golf bag with perch, put the hood of the bag over the fish, and returned all of the clubs to the bag.

Al Sutphin then drove the golf bag to the train station in Kingston and put the clubs on a very slow train across Canada and eventually to Hinsdale, Illinois.

It smelled so terrible when the golf bag arrived in Chicago on a hot summer day that Bill Tobin couldn't bring it into the house.

He couldn't figure it out. He had removed the clubs – but the odor remained. He finally threw everything out – clubs and all.

Practical jokes grew more creative!

Our young cousin, John Walker, age 24, had become a Catholic priest, and he loved the informality of Kingston vacations!

He was related on our Irish mother's side – and therefore a target for serious pranks. He was another first cousin – son of our mother's only sister, Florence.

A best friend of our mother's – since school days – was also visiting that week.

She had snow-white hair at 50 years of age and was a very proper Catholic school teacher!

As the week was winding down, it seemed that Aunt Margaret Moran (pronounced "Morn") needed a ride back to Cleveland.

It was arranged for her to ride with Father John all the way home.

That morning, Fr. John felt obligated to wear his Roman collar and his all-black priest attire!

They never realized that someone had attached a "Just married" sign to the back of their car.

The reaction as they crossed the border into the U.S. was baffling.

Why were border guards staring and laughing?

When they stopped for lunch in Watertown, N.Y., the attention of onlookers to the sign was too much, and "the game was up."

On one of our final weekends in 1950, Jane was dating Harry Leitch, from Lakewood, Ohio, and invited him to see and stay with the family at their favorite summer place – Kingston, Ontario, Canada!

On a very cool September morning, Jane, Harry and sisters and brothers decided that one last ride in the boat would be the perfect "send-off" – heavy clothes and all.

Everyone was aboard when Jane stepped from the dock to board the boat.

No one held the boat!

As Jane's foot entered the boat, Jane didn't! The boat moved away. Jane lost her balance and fell into the water between the dock and the boat!

Some jokester hollered, "Hand her the anchor on the way down!"

In reminiscing, one of our favorite memories – soon after our first summer in Kingston – was a visit to Callander, Ontario, to see the Dionne quintuplets.

They had been born on our brother Jimmy's second birthday – May 28, 1934.

The Canadian newspapers were covering every move they made, and, finally, the Canadian government took over and controlled their lives.

A big pavilion-type nursery was constructed, with a winding walkway around the entire building, for viewing – through glass walls – Annette, Yvonne, Cecile, Emilie, and Marie at play.

We talked about it all our remaining summers, and Alberta still treasures her "Quints in a Basket" – each in matching outfits of a different pastel color.

However, we grew up to feel sorry for the entire family.

Our heart-felt farewell was underlined by a last trip to Boldt Castle on Heart Island – one of the famous Thousand Islands in the St. Lawrence Seaway.

Its history was born of tragedy. Mr. Boldt had built a magnificent stone castle for his beloved wife, but she died without ever living there or seeing it finished. It remains unfinished to this day.

There is enough beauty and architectural wonders to keep thousands of tourists coming to gaze there – year after year!

The Thousand Islands remain the perfect summer adventure! There were Braden Sutphin summers, too, when the Sutphin sisters took turns in Cleveland and learned the hard truth about working for a dynamo called "Dad!"

*Be available*" meant a 24/7 obligation in case "something came up." Something always found a way of coming up!

To cover that eventuality, Al Sutphin held an obligatory meeting every evening at 6 p.m. in his office.

The "meeting" involved the presence of all Arena managers – box office, group ticket sales, food and liquor, publicity and promotion, employee training, ice engineer, and Norbert Stein, the "Go-to Guy."

The meeting lasted an hour before anyone went home – except Norbert, who never seemed to go home.

Each manager was then given a chance to report on yesterday's assignments that had to have been carried out that day (believe me).

At that point, tomorrow's job was then assigned.

There were no instructions, no guidelines. You were hired because you knew your job – so do your job!

Here was a Boss who knew what guaranteed success – smart people doing a good job!

If any of us had borrowed $1,000,000 and was in the process of paying back the investors and the insurance company who made the loan, wouldn't we have been uptight and dedicated to achieving success?

We certainly thought so, and were amazed at Al Sutphin's capacity for hard work – and the energy to micromanage his people 24/7!

As Jane represented Mrs. Robertson at her first 6 p.m. meeting, she heard her Dad say, "We will now assign the Publicity Department the job of the 'four-sheet placement.' Report success tomorrow night at 6 p.m."

Our Dad might as well have been speaking his WWI French!

Innocent Jane asked, "What are four-sheets?"

Norbert, as always, saved the day. He sent Jane to the Event Manager, who installs the 4' x 8' weather-proofed, colored posters of coming Arena attractions. They are placed – as planned – on both sides of the street all along Euclid Avenue.

When Jane – at her first meeting – had asked her Dad, "What are four-sheets?" there was a stunned silence from all the managers.

At the meeting the following night, no one expected to see Jane again – ever.

Norbert sat hiding a grin while Jane reported that "the four-sheets will all be installed on Euclid Avenue by the end of the week!"

Further, Beattie's Jewelry Store on Euclid Avenue at E. 12th Street was featuring in their front window a glittering ice-skating princess – dressed in miniature diamonds, sapphires and rubies – promoting the opening of the Ice Capades at the Cleveland Arena. The year was 1944.

The decade of the 40s had found the Sutphin family *on the move*!

Our lives were full and adventures were hard to believe, because they all involved things we had never done before – and loved doing!

People – from very different walks of life! We lived with them – as our guests – and became enriched by their presence in our lives.

There were sportswriters with Cleveland and Toronto newspapers. The Cleveland Press' Carl Shatto was a frequent guest. He once tried to avoid another lengthy Baron hockey practice by saying, "When you find a new way to practice, call me."

There were Hoynes cousins, and Conways, and printer friends, and pals from school, and (best of all) that Cook family – three generations strong!

As we said goodbye to twelve summers and one last swim to Pitcairn Island (facing us – one mile away – across the St. Lawrence River), we also thought of all those German officers who escaped in our Chris Craft and the surveillance of the Canadian officers who swarmed our waterfront – one very exciting day – to bring the war to our cottage door and to find those German prisoners!

Back in Cleveland, we were engaged in our last duties as "Arena kids." Being "available" belonged to a different world!

A man named Bernard "Buddy" E. Rand changed all that.

He was involved in the sale of the Arena in 1949, when our Dad knew that it was the "right time."

Our Dad had done it all! Our mother had done it all with him – rosaries and all!

Prayers were still a daily force for good, but now it was for health, happiness, and visits with what was to become 28 grandchildren.

Those Sutphin "Arena kids" had one last duty to perform. They raced in cars all over Ohio to retrieve the signed Debentures from the investors, so the Bonds could be redeemed – at full face value.

By late June of 1949, Al Sutphin was finally doing what he had dreamed of for years.

He was aboard the Queen Mary, sailing with those "very available" four daughters – now 26, 24, 22, and 20.

They were to learn the wonders of Europe and the essence of friendship with his war buddy, Pierre Gillot, and the entire Gillot family.

The Calvados was waiting at the Café du Commerce in Pierrefitte, France.

It is 11 a.m., and nobody is saying anything but "Salud!"

Notes: Our Dad returned every other year for a visit with Pierre and the Gillot family for the rest of his life. Pierre understood every word of our Dad's WWI French. "Au revoir" for them occurred as they turned 76, and Pierre Gillot died!

Before the marriages begin in the decade of the 50s, we need to relive the Sutphin children's school years.

As Mary Elizabeth started school, St. Ann did not have a kindergarten. Three blocks away, Fairfax public school did.

Mary attended Fairfax for one year – escorted to school by nurse-girl, Rosie. She then spent first through eighth grades at St. Ann School, graduating in 1937.

Mary loved sports and earning money! She considered both worthy challenges.

At home on Derbyshire Road, she was the self-appointed manager – every summer – of all baseball games played on the vacant lot on the corner of Kent and Derbyshire Roads.

She oversaw all baseball "choose up sides."

No one chose her sister, Jane, until last, but both sides wanted sister, Carolyn, a natural-born hitter and base-stealer!

Alberta was the youngest, at five years old, so she had to cover the outfield – allowing many a home run!

All winter on the hill – Norfolk and Derbyshire – Mary E. arranged toboggan rides for all the neighbors. It was Mary E.'s toboggan!

As the Arena expanded our horizons, ice skating sessions attracted the Cleveland Skating Club, who was constructing a brand-new and beautiful ice rink at Shaker Square.

Mary E. became fast friends with several Laurel School families, such as the Charles Gales and the Robert Struvens, who became "forever" friends.

The more Mary E.'s new friends talked of intramural sports at Laurel School – field hockey, tennis, baseball, and basketball – the more Mary E. knew she had to find a way to talk her Dad into allowing her to attend a private prep school.

Working at Braden Sutphin Ink was the answer. It encouraged her business skills. She earned the $500.00-a-year tuition – in the shipping room – in time to enter Laurel's Upper School in 1937.

With the Great Depression, enrollment was down. There were three more sisters, and all became graduates of Braden Sutphin Ink's shipping room and Laurel School's 1941, 1943, 1945, and 1947 classes! Our Dad attended every sporting event that he could possibly work into his schedule – and loved it all!

Mary E.'s "baseball throw" record stood for many years – a record that made her Dad beam – right along with all her sisters, who envied her!

Florence Jane always found life a little different.

First of all, "Florence" was never used – ever!

When she walked to Fairfax with sister Mary E. (when Jane was too young to start school) and had to go back home with nurse Rosie, she didn't take it well!

Rosie soon learned that if they stopped at Stock's Candy Store at Fairmount and Cedar, Jane became an angel.

## LESSON: EVERYONE HAS THEIR PRICE!

The Catholic Diocese was constructing Beaumont Catholic School for girls when Jane was to graduate in 1939 from St. Ann.

She had already had several incidents along the years.

In first grade, she was punished for talking in class and kept from recess. Recess meant a bathroom break. Jane didn't get one! When class resumed, there was a puddle under Jane's desk. The humiliation was enormous when one of her male classmates was instructed "to get a mop."

At 90 years old now, Jane still blushes.

In third grade, there was a whole new lesson to learn about boys.

"First Fridays" meant Mass for all students and orange juice and doughnuts – in the cafeteria – before classes began.

As Jane reached her third-grade room, she was very self-conscious. She was wearing wire-rim glasses – for the very first time – and hoped no one would notice!

Not so Tony DeSanto!

He shouted out to the entire class, "Hi, there, four eyes!" and punched her so hard in the solar plexus that all the air was knocked out, and she and the glasses fell to the floor.

Now that she thinks about it, maybe he – in first grade – was the boy who had to "get the mop."

By seventh grade, Jane had a resentment involving her rotation in the family!

She was never going to be *first*! Every second child knows that from day one! But "having her turn" became a cause celebre. Mary E. got dolls and attention from grandparents, who gave special treats!

At twelve, Mary E. was first to have her family's very straight hair permanent-waved and her "Mary Jane" patent-leather, little girl's shoes replaced with low, Cuban-heeled pumps.

Jane, in the meantime, anxiously awaited *her* turn.

It became an obsession!

Her turn was next. Her turn. Her turn next. *Her turn*!

When her turn came, it included her sister, Carolyn.

They went to the beauty parlor *together*. The shoe store had those coveted pumps in Carolyn's size, also!

Where did Jane's *turn* go?

Her mother tried to reason with her. Carolyn had grown as tall as Jane. They looked exactly the same age.

And Mom needed a break! "Doing" for each and all four needy little girls was tiring!

Jane saw only injustice rear its ugly head! For the rest of her life, she found "causes" that needed correcting, and by Jove, she was going to correct them!

In high school, Jane discovered the answer to all the ills of human behavior in three little words: "Stamp out hormones."

In 1939, when Beaumont was still under construction, St. Ann initiated a ninth grade to hold over the eighth-grade girls who might gravitate to Cleveland Heights High School.

At St. Ann, a big change occurred! All high school curriculums were offered in different classrooms around the school.

Rather than "low man" in a regular freshman high school rotation, these first-time "high schoolers" were the Big Guys – all seven girls and five boys.

Jane then followed Mary E. to Laurel School as a sophomore- both sisters *together* having that singular experience!

Mary E. and Carolyn found immediate popularity because of their athletic abilities.

Jane left St. Ann School with two gifts:

1. An abiding belief that her family is in God's protective custody.
2. A set of tools (from business math class) – low overhead and cash flow.

From Laurel – Friendships that have lasted seventy-plus years.

Rowena Scott (Lahr) opened the door to intellectual curiosity, and Betty Hughes, Grace Gale, Ann Carlisle, Liz Ripley, Jackie Schreck, Mary Ellen Wier and Nancy Wykoff walked through. Among other fun pursuits, so did Jane.

From the movie "Air Force," Ro and Jane invite Charles Drake and James Brown to be their Senior Prom escorts. With autographed pictures – they decline!

Now, as the saying goes, "We saved the best for last."

Alberta Ernestine is the fourth and final *girl*.

She has chestnut brown curls and big brown eyes, an engaging smile, and a sunny disposition – she never makes waves!

She is an immediate favorite of our Dad! (It helped that he was numb!) When we wanted our Dad's permission to do something or to go somewhere, we always sent Alberta to persuade him!

Her only failure – sleepovers. We were never permitted to sleep anywhere but under our own roof!

Nail polish and lipstick were limited – for school dances only (unless Dad was out of town).

Alberta's "ace in the hole" was her skating ability – utilized at the Arena on home game hockey nights.

Her early morning private skating lessons gave her a life of her own – often without her three big sisters. Skating was a top priority – Alberta is our own skating star! Later on, she is the superstar of married bliss!

James Hoynes Sutphin brings changes.

Our focus now was assimilating a *boy*, who was different in size, shape, interests, and expectations, into our lives every day.

Betty Cook, his nurse, led the way; but soon he was our playmate, and organized sports came first – not endless discussions of movie stars and clothes.

He was so good and fair and decent about all our "doings," that we had him marked for the religious life.

Our mother's word was final: "Your father would be crushed!"

Our father had his own imagination working.

Braden Sutphin Ink now employed two of our Dad's best boyhood friends, Bill Reiser and Albert "Mooks" Betz, who had all been together in the trenches in France in WWI and all through elementary and Central High School – always together!

As the years go by, "Who will take over?" becomes paramount!

Jimmy is it!

In 1948, at sixteen years of age, Jimmy is put on the payroll for shipping room duty. Charlie Flenders can't believe his eyes – another Sutphin after four Sutphin girls, and here comes Jimmy! He follows our lead – he is remarkable at shipping!

In 1951, Bill Reiser retires from the Akron territory, and Jimmy is given his printer friends to call on.

Jimmy is at John Carroll University. He books all of his classes for 7:30 p.m. to 10:00 p.m., so he can call on accounts in Akron during the day.

Braden Sutphin's Pennsylvania territory is being handled by a former Baron hockey player named Les Brennan. He retires to return to his Canadian home.

Our Dad tells Jimmy (in June of 1954):

1. Go to Harrisburg, Pa.
2. Find the garage where Les Brennan left the Braden Sutphin car.
3. Get the car.
4. Go to work there!

Jimmy's territory is everything east of the Susquehanna River in Pennsylvania.

He calls on printer friends and the Scotvold twins wherever he can find the Ice Follies performing for all of 1954, 1955, and 1956.

In January of 1957, Braden Sutphin Ink's western Ohio and southern Michigan salesman, Joe Yeager, moved to Rochester, N.Y., to take over for Bob Brinson.

Jimmy now covers northwest Ohio and southern Michigan until Alberta's husband, Ray Stoney, takes over that territory after managing the Braden Sutphin Farm in Ft. Myers, Florida, for twelve years.

Stoney and Alberta had moved from Bay Village, Ohio, to Ft. Myers with their one-year-old daughter, Gail, in 1951. They have added twins, Ray and Matt, and daughters, Ann, Lynn, and Elaine, all born in Ft. Myers.

(Now, in 1968, they also add a basement and a garage filled with cans of ink, and they must find a building to set up Braden Sutphin Ink's *first* branch, in Detroit, Michigan.)

Jimmy Sutphin – ever the rescuer – is now free to cover Jack Reay's territory in southern Ohio. Mr. Reay has retired.

Jimmy Sutphin covers southern Ohio from 1963 to 1967.

In 1967, Al Sutphin retires, and guess who comes inside the Braden Sutphin headquarters on East 93rd Street?

Jimmy Sutphin, of course!

He is now President of the Braden Sutphin Ink Company!

It is February, 1967.

Al Sutphin now lives full time on the Farm in Ft. Myers, Florida. He never returns to Cleveland, but is in daily touch with all aspects of Cleveland life.

He has twenty-eight grandchildren – almost all Clevelanders at birth – just as "The Champ" has directed.

Jimmy, meanwhile, is trying to lead the company – without parental support! He has an incredible task of learning "on the job." He is still calling on printer friends.

His brother, Cal, will eventually take over.

Jimmy Sutphin leaves Braden Sutphin Ink and joins NAPIM (National Association of Printing Ink Manufacturers), and remains in New Jersey from May of 1989 to September of 1997.

Now, the Rotary in Hudson, Ohio, claims Jimmy's best self. His sense of belonging – and, therefore, giving – to his community occupies his retirement years.

Parades, fundraisers, St. Mary's Catholic Church, and the family are his focus. Every Monday morning, Jimmy Sutphin joins a group of guys and gals who clean and polish St. Mary's.

He travels to University Heights to volunteer on a Founder's Committee at his alma mater, John Carroll University. He also keeps in touch with classmates who shared many an adventure at graduation time in 1954.

Albert and Mary Sutphin now have grown children – with adult ideas of whom they should be!

Their Dad may not have graduated from high school, but he believed in higher education for his four daughters and two sons – with reservations!

1. They must attend college in Cleveland.
2. They must live at home – under his roof – and ride the street car.
3. If they marry, they must marry Cleveland boys or girls, so his grandchildren will live in Cleveland!
4. He will pay for four years of college! If you dilly-dally around and haven't enough credits to graduate in four years, they will come out and go to work or pay your own way.

Mary E., Jane, and Carolyn chose Flora Stone Mather.

Alberta chose to be a "domestic goddess" and learn homemaking from an excellent teacher – her mother!

Miss Lake, Laurel School's headmistress, felt that Vassar was an ideal choice for Carolyn – until she met Al Sutphin, whose mind centered on Cleveland! Miss Lake had no reason to doubt her persuasive skills with difficult fathers. She usually won!

On the occasion of her encounter with Al Sutphin, a master of persuasion himself, she had met her match – and lost!

Carolyn Alberta Sutphin was a 1948 graduate of Flora Stone Mather College in Cleveland, Ohio having majored in Calculus, with a minor in Sociology.

Volunteering loomed large. The annual Western Reserve University book sale at the Adelbert gym became her challenge in the 1950s. She devised a method to have more books for sale. She contacted the President of Society National Bank. She convinced him to allow large painted boxes to be placed in the lobby of all Society branches (they had the most on the east and west sides of Cleveland). "Please place books here" said the signs on the boxes.

Her loyal friends became lieutenants (they picked up the books from the Society Bank – in their neighborhood – every Friday and took them to "the Captains," who took them to "the Sorters").

Their book sale wasn't the largest – eventually 70,000 books – but it was the best sorted – for easy shopping.

Carolyn gave thirty years of her life as sorter, worker, recruiter, manager, chili-maker for late nights, and all-around cheerleader.

After her death in 1993, scores of her best friends have continued on – still at the old Adelbert gym on Adelbert Road.

Her recruiting included sister, Jane, who was assigned to assist Carolyn Heller in the textbook department (the largest section, except for paperbacks) in the annual Adult Continuing Education (A.C.E.) book sale.

"Textbooks" is a category featuring Medicine (including three-pound Grey's Anatomy), Law, Engineering, Math, Nursing, and Foreign Language – to name a few.

Carolyn Heller is a tireless worker and a patient instructor – a trait running rampant in all A.C.E. volunteers.

Jane is lucky to have five years before Carolyn Heller is felled by cancer.

Marjorie Johnson takes over for Carolyn Heller. She has such an interesting history as a teacher of English in France and later as a French teacher at Hawken School and "team leader" for Continuing Education, that Jane signs up for several of her classes.

The book sale is a fundraiser for A.C.E. offered in schools, homes, libraries, retirement places – both east and west sides – and finally on the south side of Cleveland!

The classes cover Art, Science, Literature, History, Novels, The Classics – everything you have ever wanted to put into your head – after age fifty – and now a paid, first-class teacher will serve that purpose!

Every June, the classes become "summer school for adults" at Squire Valleevue Farm, in a charming building – a former pig sty – now named "The Pink Pig." Bird watching and painting are offered out-of-doors as well.

Western Reserve undergraduate students are entitled – as seniors – to a weekend in the country before graduation. This is a cherished opportunity – as the Chagrin Valley is beautiful, and the Pink Pig accommodates all your best friends!

Kathy Manos is a gifted Director of Education and Lorraine Nelson an indispensable Program Administrator, going back to all of Carolyn Sutphin's years!

Now, "textbooks" is run by Ed Golinski and Carol Casciani – a book-smart couple – who are tireless volunteers. It brings back those who have their own twenty- to forty-year histories – Joanne Blazek, Lois Hawn, Alice Walker, "Del" in Arts, and faithful, dear friends, Mary Jo Groppe and, later, Barbara Nahra.

Carolyn's sister, Jane, has taken advantage of her sister's incredible efforts and taken A.C.E. classes for seventy years, and counting.

Life-long Learning – headed now by Laura and Alvin Siegal – are new and worthy names for 90-year-old Jane to learn!

LESSON: THAT'S WHAT EDUCATION IS ALL ABOUT – LEARNING – SOMETHING THAT CHANGES YOU – ALL IN GOOD WAYS!

Mary E., always a business head with great ideas and hands to match, left Mather College after two years wasted on Chemistry (mandatory for "home design" majors). She now honed her skills at Irvin and Company at Shaker Square.

There, she not only *sold* the draperies, in emergencies she took out her handy electric drill and installed them!

Jane was intrigued! Her junior year – without Mary E. – targeted her to be the first Sutphin to have a college degree.

With tuition at $5.00 a semester hour -- $120.00 a semester – she had joined her sister working on Saturdays at the Braden Sutphin Ink Company.

Early on, all the sisters had become a four-woman blitz team in the shipping room – sending sixty-pound crates of twelve five-pound cans of ink, ready for delivery, out the door!

Later on, a trip to Ohio Bell prepared them for running the switchboard in the front office – upstairs – where they also were instructed by Dorothy Baird to write up orders and file.

Jane found herself taking a senior year Geography class on her lunch hour at the ink company in 1946.

She was at the switchboard, doing weather maps as homework, when an irate Vice President, Mr. Erikson, came rushing into the front office yelling, "Why can't I get an outside line?"

Jane had covered all the blinking lights with her map!

Earlier in her junior year, Mather's Registrar, Miss Eleanor Wells, had alerted Jane to the possibility of not being eligible for graduation in four years – 1947 – as she was six semester hours short of enough credit hours.

Horrors! It was already 1946! Miss Wells saved the day and Jane's B.A. degree in Theatre and English. She strongly suggested a once-in-a-lifetime opportunity for theatre majors.

Western Reserve University – for the summer of 1946 – would have a Straw Hat Summer Theatre program at Squire Valleevue Farm, WRU's country campus at Fairmount Blvd. in Gates Mills.

For six credit hours and six weeks, three melodramas would be mounted in a big, beautiful barn converted for theatre productions – for one summer!

Result: Jane graduated in June, 1947 – with her Flora Stone Mather classmates – in particular, her best friend from Laurel School, Rowena Scott.

After graduation, Rowena Scott married Adelbert graduate, Warren Lahr, home from the Navy Air Force in WWII. He was a gunner!

Warnie was drafted by the Cleveland Browns as a defensive back – No. 24 – and played for eleven seasons, from 1948 to 1959.

Jane follows Ro's example and marries in 1950.

Thirteen years later, Rowena and Jane had babies due *the same day* – June 21, 1963. (They had just attended their Laurel 20th Reunion on June 5!)

Nancy Louise Lahr arrived one day early: June 20, 1963.

Margaret Lindsay Leitch was already one week old – and smiling!

In 1963, the two moms were 36 and 38 years old.

Schoolmates, welcome back! Please prepare yourselves for the 50s, where the college graduates meet the returning veterans and wedding bells ring out!

## CHAPTER IV

# MARRIAGES – THE 1950S

In Lakewood, Ohio, lived three young, Protestant men who had never heard of three young, Cleveland Heights Catholic women named Jane, Carolyn, and Alberta Sutphin.

They were separated by the Cuyahoga River – culturally, geographically, and by a long car ride!

Harry Leitch, Jr., and his brother, Bob, were products of the Lakewood school system.

Raymond Edward Stoney, Jr., was also.

A quirk of fate prevented them from attending Lakewood High School together.

Harry, Jr., and Bob Leitch were parented by Harry Leitch, Sr., and Mary Rose Brennan – an Irish lass with Gaelic determination and spitfire!

She was four feet nine inches tall, and Harry, Jr. – at five feet six inches – was the apple of her eye. She looked up to him!

When a misguided Lakewood High School teacher told Mary Rose – now Mame – that her "apple" was too limited to learn Latin, Mame had her answer all ready: "The Dad and I will send him where they know how to teach Latin – the Jesuits at St. Ignatius."

This announcement challenged the Leitch household budget – St. Ignatius was $150.00 a year!

They found the money, and Harry, Jr., was a straight A student in Latin all four years, also an amazing gymnast, and shortstop on the St. Ignatius baseball team.

His size – as a gymnast – was perfect for being catapulted into the air, performing two somersaults, and landing in a wicker chair on a teammate's shoulders!

Harry – and, two years later, Bob – became the first Protestant boys to attend and graduate Jesuit St. Ignatius High School.

Their parents granted permission to have them taught the Catholic faith in Religion class when Mame declared, *"It can't hurt 'em!"*

Harry, Jr.'s father – as noted – was an engineer for the vast Pickands Mather Great Lakes shipping empire. He spent eight months away every year on an oil tanker on the Great Lakes.

In late 1918 – 1919, he was "coming off the Lakes" for the four-month winter hiatus. As he entered the Pickands Mather office in Buffalo, N.Y., he noticed a small, very pretty Irish lass, named Mary Rose Brennan.

He couldn't be married and sail away eight months a year!

He chose marriage, a home in Lakewood, and a job as engineer for The City Ice Company, making ice for the Winterhurst skating rink in Lakewood and also for home delivery.

Harry and Mary Rose had bought a small three-bedroom, one-bath home – with a large front porch.

The B & O Railroad ran a block behind their home on Hazelwood Avenue, off Clarence Avenue, just north of Detroit Road.

Their home cost $4,000 in 1920. It was a struggle when Harry, Jr., arrived – born at home – on April 7, 1921.

He was followed by red-haired Robert Andrew – also born at home – on February 24, 1924.

Both parents were in their thirties!

Mame loved those boys, while Harry, Sr. – a quiet man – worked hard, and found early Sunday morning golf his great escape!

Upon graduation from St. Ignatius in 1939, Harry, Jr. – encouraged by Fr. Sullivan, his religion teacher and *baseball coach* – had found himself at the Boston Braves spring training camp – begging manager, Casey Stengel, for a chance at shortstop!

Casey Stengel growled, "You're only five feet six and 118 pounds, Harry! Go home, put some weight on, grow a little, and come back in a year!"

In that year, Harry's father was killed by the train that ran behind their house in Lakewood. The signal had not announced the arrival of a second train – going in the opposite direction – and the gate had gone up, signaling that passage was allowed.

In an eerie coincidence, both Harry and Bob Leitch were about to become acquainted with Ray Stoney – also fatherless.

The rules of voluntary conscription dictated that an "only remaining son" could not be drafted. Both mothers let their remaining sons go to war!

Bob Leitch and Ray Stoney will be introduced to George Patton's Third Army in Bastogne, Belgium.

Raymond Edward Stoney, Jr., is an all-time "west sider."

His grandfather, John Taylor Stoney, emigrated from England and created the Stoney Foundry and Engineering Company.

Ray lived near the lake with his father, Ray, Sr., his mother, Pearl, and her two unmarried sisters, Ann and Eve. Older brother, Jack, was his constant companion and best friend.

Upon graduation from Lakewood High School, Ray, Jr., was happily driving a cement truck for the Dover Cement Company – and loving it!

Death and a war changed everything! Ray, Jr. – in his senior year – came home to find his Dad dead in the garage, from a heart attack!

The Stoney family moved to Munn Road. Mame Leitch was rearing her two boys alone on Hazelwood Avenue.

By 1942, Harry Leitch, Jr., had joined the Navy. Being just five feet six, he was a candidate for submarine duty, and was studying Morse Code and waiting in Miami Beach to be assigned.

A foot disease – called "jungle rot" by the Navy doctor – kept Harry hospitalized for weeks. He was sent – finally – to the University of Miami for college classes in naval navigation. Then to Georgia Tech for more classes!

It was rumored that a red-headed WAVE was a big part of Harry's education!

Master Sergeant Bob Leitch and Private First Class Ray Stoney – unknown to one another – were assigned to General George Patton's Third

Army, rushing – hell bent – for Bastogne, Belgium, and the infamous Battle of the Bulge.

It is to be their Christmas present in 1944. They are each twenty years old!

Bob is a signalman assigned to report enemy positions – by Morse Code – from "the front."

Ray (Stoney) is driving a truck (the army has utilized his skills). He transports every manner of supplies – food, ammunition, some clothing – to those fast-moving troops rushing toward the biggest and almost final battle of World War II.

He also brings back those who have served their "last full measure of devotion." [From the Gettysburg Address] (Stoney never mentioned this part of his war job for many years after WWII.)

As the war ends in Europe in May 1945, Ray is held in France while those who served longer are mustered out first!

He returns home for a 30-day furlough to find that he is assigned to a troop ship for the invasion of Japan.

President Harry Truman saves these American men, who now find themselves *not* in an invasion force, but serving as an occupation army in Japan for a six-month tour of duty.

Bob Leitch, thinking that his war is finally over, joins the Army Reserves to pal around – post war – with his buddies!

He has met and married Carolyn Sutphin in June of 1951 – when his entire army unit is called up and sent to Alexandria, Louisiana, for training for duty in the Korean War!

Their honeymoon is spent on an Army base, housed in a former chicken coop with a dirt floor and running water only in the bathroom – none in the kitchen. He has sworn Carolyn to secrecy about their "romantic" first months of married bliss.

It is one hundred degrees – both temperature and humidity – by 5:00 a.m. daily. Bob's troop assignment is cancelled!

Many years later, as Jane looks back at her family's military history, she is proud to realize that every time her country needed her family, a Sutphin or Hoynes family member answered the call.

In the Revolutionary War, it was a farmer named William Sutphin, newly arrived from Zutphen, Holland, The Netherlands. (1776 – 1778)

In the Civil War, Mary Hoynes' Sutphin grandfather, Oscar Brownell, served in the battlefield as a surgeon. (1861 – 1864)

Albert Claude Sutphin and his entire neighborhood and his brother-in-law, Dan Hoynes, served in the trenches in France in WWI. (1917 – 1918)

World War II found Jane's husband, Harry Leitch, in the Navy.

Her brother-in-law, Bob Leitch, in the Army and Battle of the Bulge, was called to Korea, but did not serve there. Alberta's husband, Ray Stoney, was in the Army at the Battle of the Bulge and the occupation of Japan.

Jane and Harry's daughter, Mary Dana, marries Elmer Fisher, a Marine home from Viet Nam. Their daughter, Heather, marries an Air Force sergeant, Rob Ernst, who serves five tours of duty – first in Germany, then in Iraq and Afghanistan. Sergeant Rob Ernst retired after twenty years of Air Force duty! Rob and Heather – not together now – have a son, Matthew Ernst, born when Rob and Heather served in Alt Hornbach, Germany.

Matt is a true sportsman – baseball and basketball are his first choices.

He believes that he can be the best at anything he tackles!

As of November 1, 2014, he has a brand-new challenge – at 25, he is a new husband!

Jennifer Loman met Matthew Ernst at Campbell College in North Carolina. They have now graduated – Jennifer, with a teaching degree, and Matt in Criminal Justice. After Jennifer's first year of teaching, she was named "Teacher of the Year!" Matt believes that criminal justice should begin on a policeman's beat.

He is now ready to follow his Dad, Rob, into the military life. He has applied. He would be the seventh generation since the Revolutionary War to serve his country.

## LESSON: SINCE THE U.S.A. NEVER RUNS OUT OF ENEMIES – BE READY!

When Harry Leitch met Jane Sutphin, she was working for the Cleveland Arena, selling two-for-one professional basketball tickets for the new Cleveland Rebels. These two-for-one tickets were for the entire new season. Her targets were Cleveland Catholic industries which had companies big enough to have sales managers, long customer lists, and salesmen trained to make their customer friends happy.

Jane's Dad, Al Sutphin, had given Jane a list of John Carroll University alums who owned Cleveland companies. Her Dad said, "You've attended Catholic St. Ann's and know many of these families from church. It should give you an entrance!"

Jane began, alphabetically, with Ames Manufacturing. By the time she reached Union Carbide, she found her grandfather, "Gaga" Sutphin, in the waiting room about to sell paper for his employer, Central Ohio Paper Co. Amazingly enough, there was also her father waiting to sell ink to the ink buyer, and there was Jane – the third generation of Sutphin salesman – with her Basketball Association of America tickets, and with her father and grandfather in the cheering section!

Her very next call – alphabetically speaking – was United Screw and Bolt Corp., owned by the Kramer brothers, Carl and Gene. Jane asked the receptionist for Mr. Gene Kramer – on her list as Sales Manager. When Mr. Kramer appeared, Jane was struck by his good looks. He was six feet one, in great shape, with silver gray hair framing a tanned, youthful face. Jane warmed to her task!

He liked the idea of two-for-one season tickets to benefit his sales force, taking customer friends to an exciting new sport. Baron hockey games had been sold out for years. Now, national basketball would be an "edge" in selling nuts and bolts.

As Mr. Kramer contemplated the purchase of *six* season tickets – the biggest sale that Jane had made – they were rudely interrupted by a short young man, who introduced himself as Harry Leitch.

He had a "beef" with the Cleveland Arena. When he had requested season tickets for Baron hockey games, the Arena had not even responded to his request.

Jane explained that Baron hockey games were sold out from one season to the next and that she was offering a great opportunity to be in on the ground floor of a growing new sport – the Basketball Association of America – at a cost-saving advantage.

Mr. Kramer hesitated!

Jane took an instant dislike to Mr. Leitch. Mr. Leitch began calling Miss Sutphin for ringside tickets for boxing matches and offers for lunch after the Arena box office now honored his request for two season tickets for Baron hockey games. Jane refused lunch!

The Kramer family had offered Harry a job – as George's best friend – after the War. Both had been in the Navy.

Harry had been with United Screw and Bolt for eleven years. They had taught Harry everything from the factory furnace, to the office, to sales on the road.

Since Alberta's wedding had been an entire year in the planning, Harry and Bob Leitch were invited to be groomsmen.

Meanwhile, brother Jimmy, also a groomsman, had his own big event in the planning. "Club Sutphin" was his inspiration for a graduation party. He walked into the locker room at University School and invited everybody he saw to his home on Berkshire Road. It was the day before his sister Alberta's wedding to Ray Stoney, Jr.

Jimmy had a lot to learn.

First, do not announce a party to a world of eighteen-year-olds!

By dawn, all of the champagne for the Sutphin-Stoney wedding had been found in the basement – and consumed! Furniture had been broken by revelers that Jimmy had never seen before, and his Dad, Al Sutphin, declared, "Club Sutphin has been opened and now closed – forever!"

The next morning, Jim awakens with evidence of too much fun and "price-paying" pain! As he ponders his groomsman tuxedo and reminds himself that he will be *on the altar* serving as an usher for the very first wedding in this big family, he reaches for another aspirin.

The groom's family – the Ray Stoneys, from Lakewood – are strangers in a strange land!

The groom, Ray Stoney, is a convert. His family have never been in a Catholic Church. His mother, Pearl, and her sisters, Anne and Eve, and Ray's brother, Jack, decide that watching the bride's side is their only hope!

They watch. "Oh, they're up now; we must get up." The Stoney family gets up.

Too late. "The Catholics are down."

The Stoneys flop down!

"Oh, the bride's side is up again!"

The Protestants' side is down.

Up and down – for an hour's Mass – or mess!

Earlier, Jimmy's mother had reminded him that he cannot eat or drink anything *before* the ceremony, as he will be having Holy Communion on the altar, and must fast.

Jimmy faints on the altar during the wedding, and he is carried off!

Jane – in the meantime – is also in a state! She cries out loud through the entire ceremony! She cannot accept Alberta's decision to "break up" the four sisters for something as mundane as marriage!

**LESSON: RAY AND ALBERTA STAY MARRIED FOR SIXTY-FOUR YEARS. SOMEBODY GOT IT RIGHT!**

(Meanwhile, Jane had convinced Nate Dolan, head of the Arena box office, that Harry Leitch stood in the way of Mr. Gene Kramer buying six season tickets to basketball!)

Jane's Dad had learned from his brother-in-law, Paul Hoynes (Mary's brother), who attended every Notre Dame football game, that the Kramers were always on the same train to South Bend, Indiana, as he was. He knew them well!

Jane – the very next Saturday – was booked on the "Notre Dame Special" train to South Bend for the Notre Dame/Michigan State game.

She joined Carl and Gene Kramer and her uncle, Paul, and had a rollicking good time up and back again to Cleveland on October 9, 1948. The score was Notre Dame, 26; Michigan State, 7!

Mr. Gene Kramer bought *eight* season tickets – for half price – and helped launch The Rebels basketball at the Cleveland Arena in the late 1940s!

Jane married Harry Leitch on November 3, 1950, and honeymooned in the bleachers that weekend – in the pouring rain – at the Notre Dame/Navy game.

They had dinner after the game at Fisher Rohr's restaurant at Sixth and Short Vincent. Chuck Rohr was married to Gene Kramer's sister, Loretta (Sis).

Harry invited three couples back to their $8.00 room at the Aurora Treadway Inn. They came and stayed till dawn.

Jane insisted that they attend Mass at St. Rita's in Solon, Ohio, at 10:00 a.m. Sunday morning!

They had been married in St. Ann's "priest house." Father Powers would not allow a Catholic and a Presbyterian to be married in the church!

Jesuit Father Sullivan – from St. Ignatius – officiated!

It was a sleety, wet, icy night. As a surprise, Ro and Warnie Lahr attended with ten Leitch and Sutphin family members.

They enjoyed a lobster dinner (no meat – it was a Friday night) at Jane's home on Berkshire Road.

Jane's grandfather, Gaga, attended. Carolyn stood up for Jane. Bob Leitch was in Louisiana with the Army. He was upset that Harry would get married without his only brother as best man. George Kramer – Gene's youngest brother – stood up for Harry.

Mame Leitch was so relieved that it was a simple ceremony; she had a wonderful evening with Jane's grandfather, Jane's parents, and getting acquainted with all of Jane's sisters and brothers in an informal setting.

Jane's Dad said, "Best wedding yet!" The honeymooners were gone by 9:30 p.m. – after a 7:00 ceremony and 8:00 dinner – and the family were engaged in their favorite pastime, 500 rummy, by 9:45 p.m.

An interesting aside!

In the car – on the way to Aurora, Ohio – Jane asked Harry where his money was. What bank?

He was thirty years old, and had worked for eleven years at United Screw. Ray Stoney had a small bank account, so sister Alberta seemed secure! How naïve!

Harry was surprised at the question. His response startled Jane: "I have never had a bank account. I earn it, and I spend it!"

It was Jane's turn to be startled! She had saved $3,000 from her job with the New Neighbor's League, and was still gainfully employed there as a representative, calling on out-of-towners newly relocated to the Cleveland scene. She was sponsored by businesses that needed these very new customers.

Harry then reached into his pocket – while driving – and pulled out all his cash. It amounted to two twenties and a ten-dollar bill. As he tossed them into her lap, Jane declared, "Our apartment is $50 a month. What are you planning on doing for money?"

Harry responded, "I'll earn it – period!"

Jane never doubted he would! He kept his word in spades! – and diapers!

Their first baby – and first grand*son*, Timothy Brownell Leitch – arrived a week early – nine months later – on July 29, 1951.

Amazingly, Gene and Margaret Kramer had their eighth and final child, Mark, on the exact same day and same time as Harry and Jane's *Tim* – their first.

Alberta and Ray Stoney had already blessed our parents with their very first grandchild – Gail Suzanne Stoney – a blond, blue-eyed, dear little girl, who grew up fast, and invited her first cousin, Tim Leitch, to accompany her to her senior prom – eighteen years later.

They have both represented the Braden Sutphin Ink Company – Gail, at the Detroit, Michigan, branch – and Tim, at company headquarters at East 93rd and Aetna, Cleveland, Ohio. Each is approaching their fortieth year, and counting.

Jane's sister, Carolyn, met Bob Leitch almost by accident.

Jane was "seeing someone" when Harry Leitch was looking for someone to attend the hockey games he now had season tickets for – at the Arena.

Carolyn had just broken up with a Beta fraternity guy she had been dating – who was worried about her Catholic religion.

She agreed to attend a few Baron hockey games with Harry.

At some point, Harry took her home to meet his mother, Mame. Bob was at home!

Bob wore glasses and read a lot of books. He was an electrical engineer, and had graduated from John Carroll University (after the War, on the G.I. Bill). He now had eight years of Jesuit education.

Carolyn wore glasses, read a lot of books, and liked serious young people who weren't worried about her Catholic religion.

Jane married Harry because she had fun listening to music in bars. It seemed Jane wasn't thirsty. Harry was! Jane did have a heightened appreciation of the outrageous! Harry fit perfectly!

Carolyn married Bob Leitch because he shared her religious values and didn't drink a lot! Not in a hurry, Bob converted (to Catholicism) on their fortieth wedding anniversary.

They were married on June 12, 1951, just one year after Alberta and Ray, and seven months after Jane and Harry.

Carolyn believed in being married – at the altar! She chose Fr. Wilson's beautiful Catholic Church, St. Peter's, at Superior and E. 26th Street.

Alberta and Carolyn each chose their wedding receptions to be celebrated at home – in the yard on Berkshire Road. Mary E. stood up for both Alberta and Carolyn in the same dress – one year apart!

Seventy-five guests seemed a lot to Jane – who always preferred her ten dearest family members to be enough celebrants.

Al Sutphin had dictated their futures by insisting on college in Cleveland (while living at home), marrying Cleveland boys, and having seventeen grandchildren (*What?*) in the decade of the 50s.

Alberta and Ray Stoney had Gail, identical twin boys, Ray Jr. and Matt, and three little sisters for Gail – Ann, Lynn, and Elaine.

Jane and Harry tied the number of six with Tim, Mary Dana, Harry Albert (Hal), Bill Brady, Katy Jane, and Margaret!

Carolyn and Bob welcomed Jeff, Rob, Carolyn, Jim and Dan. They settled with their five on W. Melrose in Westlake, Ohio.

Jane's children were born on all the *odd* years of the Fifties.

Carolyn's were born on all the *even* years of the Fifties.

One visit to see the grandparents in Ft. Myers included all of Jane's and Carolyn's children that year – ten children up to age ten.

Those crafty Leitch boys backed out at the airport – and stayed home to play golf in Cleveland! (And have a few rounds at their favorite watering holes.)

Jane and Carolyn should have remembered how the Leitch boys – home from the War, on picnics – had sent Morse Code messages on beer cans, using their class rings, and laughing at their secret messages to one another!

LESSON: THIS WAS NO PICNIC!

All weddings are finished now for seven years! Our Dad has declared Mary E. too smart to marry and ruin a great business career. Mary E. agrees. Being Aunt Mary to seventeen nieces and nephews is a career in itself!

By the late 1950s, our good brother, Jimmy, had become an amateur photographer – to the point of creating a "dark room" in the basement on Berkshire Road.

Taking advantage of the convenience of Shaker Square's Camera Craft store led to his meeting – by chance – Louise Dolence. She was Camera Craft's bookkeeper, and was always behind the scenes in her office. One fateful day – short of help – Louise was out front serving customers!

Jimmy was a customer – buying his usual rolls of film. Louise, being very pretty and very efficient, led to his getting to know her better!

She is the youngest of ten children, born on a farm in Lisbon, Ohio. Her older sisters, Ann and Helen, had married Marines stationed in Morocco at the end of World War II.

Louise was pals with her closest sisters, Margie and Dorothy. They had trudged together through stormy winters to a one-room school house two miles from home – kindergarten through eighth grade.

Just after the War, they made an incredible journey! Margie and Louise visited Ann and Helen in Morocco, and then journeyed on to Kranz, Slovenia – now Yugoslavia – to visit their mother's homeland.

It was an eye-opener for us to meet – and to admire – two very independent sisters, sharing a lovely apartment at Shaker Square that was furnished with handsome acquisitions – all on their own!

They had created a life, without all the parental influences that we endured, and to have that life – so full of exotic travels and self-confidence – was a whole new dynamic for us Sutphin sisters.

Louise said, "Morocco was the most foreign place there is!"

Jane woke up!

A person could be anyone, come from anywhere, and make a life that works just fine – if one had vision and energy and faith in oneself.

Our amazing parents introduced us to challenges that our friends could not imagine.

Now, we had marriages that taught their own lessons, but had we learned the right lessons that would enable us to live and thrive apart from our roots?

LESSON: WE'LL SEE!

Something entirely new was happening!

Our first "baby" brother, Jimmy, was taking unto himself a life and a wife!

As Jimmy's wedding day approaches, Al Sutphin realizes an unknown element has entered the picture – a *daughter-in-law*!

Louise Dolence, now of Salem, Ohio, has ideas of her own that must be considered – even honored!

Louise is uncomfortable at the thought of a "Sutphin Extravaganza" wedding. She plans a simple – family only – Mass at Our Lady of Peace Catholic Church and a simple, small reception at the Alcazar Hotel.

Jimmy agrees!

They want to be financially involved as well.

Louise has lived independently of her big family – except for sisters, Dorothy and Margie – for a number of years, and feels in charge of her future!

Her future father-in-law has a plan!

Jimmy's "Bachelor Dinner" will answer Al Sutphin's need for an "extravaganza." It will be held at the Allerton Hotel ballroom in downtown Cleveland, at E. 13th and Chester Avenue.

Five hundred of his closest friends will attend! (Everyone he meets becomes a "closest friend.")

The table arrangement is unheard of: Jimmy's table will sit *alone* on the ballroom floor – with Jimmy!

Surrounding his table will be three tiers of tables – around the entire room – floor to ceiling.

Entertainment will be supplied by friends and family members – with poems and jokes – the more outrageous the better!

All of his University High School classmates and also college friends from John Carroll are included!

All of his printer friends will be invited and will attend – in large numbers!

Al Sutphin – father of the groom – has kept his word!

On September 13, 1958, a *small* family-only wedding will be celebrated, joining Louise Dolence and James Hoynes Sutphin in Holy Matrimony.

Our Lady of Peace is a beautiful setting!

It is a perfect late-summer day.

Both families smiled a lot and wondered at how different they were: Jimmy, outgoing – and Louise, reserved and cautious.

Louise was beautiful in a ballet-length white satin gown. Fun sister, Margie, stood up as Maid of Honor, and their brother, Bill Dolence, gave Louise away.

Guess who now ruled as the only father-in-law in four new households? Albert Sutphin! Harry and Bob Leitch, Ray Stoney, and Louise Dolence had all lost their Dads.

Sister, Alberta, and her husband, Ray Stoney, have come from Ft. Myers, Florida. Jimmy's Cleveland sisters, Carolyn (Bob Leitch) and Jane (Harry Leitch), with Alberta and Ray, now each have four children under seven years old – 12 – so far!

What was to be a quiet, refined reception at the Alcazar Hotel is a little "out of hand" when all the younger guests discover the Spanish-style pool in the front lobby of the hotel.

Meanwhile, Ray Stoney – brother-in-law – has disabled the honeymoon car, so Louise and Jimmy can't take off for Oglebay Park in southern Ohio. Our mother learns of this and soon makes all systems go by demanding that Ray rehabilitate the car.

Louise and Jimmy take off to begin 56 years of wedded bliss in Brecksville, Ohio; Akron, Ohio; Ridgewood, New Jersey; and Hudson, Ohio, in retirement.

Jimmy mastered the art of explanation. Louise mastered the art of putting-on-a-good-face-until-we-get-home.

We all loved Louise! She looked like Grace Kelly – which none of us had managed to achieve. (Carolyn came closest.)

She accepted four very new, older sisters-in-law with humor and patience and became "a very good egg."

When Jimmy knelt at the altar with a price tag of $2.99 glued to the sole of his shoe – *for all to see* – she forgave Cal, thinking that the best man had to be responsible.

Louise had the wrong man! Her new father-in-law's best-of-all-time assistant, Norbert Stein, was the "sole" culprit!

As we approach the 60s, the Sutphin girls' first-borns are old enough to be involved.

Jane hopes the same is true of her readers!

*Young Al & Family (1910)*

Standing, l. to r., Will Clark (uncle), Carey Clark (aunt),
Ernie Sutphen, Al, Ethel Sutphen (aunt, Ernie's sister), seated
l. to r., Edna Sutphen (aunt, Ernie's sister), Louise Sutphen
(grandmother), Elizabeth Pearl Thayer Sutphen (mother)

*The Hoynes Family, circa 1900*
*(Back row, standing, l. to r., Mary, Florence, Daniel, Paul*
*front row, seated, l. to r., Micheal, Dennis, Florence)*

Back row, standing, l. to r., Mary, Florence, Daniel, Paul,
front row, seated, l. to r., Michael, Dennis, Florence

*The Sutphin-Hoynes wedding party (1922)*

Albert Claude Sutphin and Mary Althea Hoynes wedding
day, August 14, 1922, St.Philomenia's Catholic Church

*The Arena ice mosaic*

Cleveland Arena Ice Follies opening night. November 10, 1937

*The Farm at Ft. Myers*

Main house and dock, Braden Sutphin Farm, Ft. Myers, Florida
1940- 1995

Grandson's baseball team with Champ, 50th Anniversary,
August 14, 1972. Terry Park in Ft. Myers, Florida

1958- All family members and three married
daughters with 12 growing grandchildren

Put-In-Bay, Ohio, 2013 Bay Bash Reunion, 62 attendees

# CHAPTER V

# THE 1960S

Many young students in the U.S.A. in the 1960s called civil disobedience their personal life-style.

What originated at Berkley, when students and teachers took over the administration building, culminated on May 4, 1970, at Kent State University when four unarmed students were gunned down by Ohio National Guardsmen.

It sent shock waves and enough citizen outrage to halt further student excesses and police overreaction on unarmed young Americans!

This nightmare was sparked by an ill-conceived Federal government's immersing itself in a war in far-away Vietnam.

This war snared a young Marine, a future member of the Al and Mary Sutphin family, named Elmer Fisher.

He married Jane Sutphin and Harry Leitch's daughter, Mary, and soon created first-time great-grandparents, Al and Mary Sutphin, and first-time, unexpected, grandparents of Jane and Harry.

Elmer, along with his fellow Marines, returned home unheralded and very different from the young boys who went to Vietnam to stop Communism from spreading all over Asia.

Now, welcome Heather Anne Fisher, born September 2, 1972, in South Euclid, Ohio. She is a bright, loving, attention-getting, brown-eyed blond with a winning personality!

Jane Sutphin Leitch, meanwhile, had caught the volunteer-to-do-good bug and had reacted to a <u>Cleveland Plain Dealer</u> article drawing attention to a rat-infested, east side, Hough Avenue neighborhood. A very charismatic young priest, newly assigned from Puerto Rico, was now pastor of a new and mainly Hispanic parish, named Our Lady of Fatima.

He was quoted in the article as saying that "the rats multiply and the men decay" here on Hough Avenue!

This blighted, underserved community was the home of the Cleveland Indians' old League Park, a once proud gathering place for professional big league baseball.

Father Albert's arrival was soon co-sponsored with a St. Vincent Charity Hospital nursing nun, Sr. Henrietta, who had aspired to foreign missions but was assigned – at 70 – to a mission much closer to home, a mile away from the hospital at E. 22nd and Chester Avenue.

A convent was soon opened, and daily visits to needy families brought spiritual guidance, proper nutrition, health care, and Saturday remedial Math and English classes for floundering students.

Concerned mothers from east side parishes were soon recruited from Gesu and St. Ann's (to name a couple), and they became Sr. Henrietta's "army" – going weekly to attend to the very needy and broken families.

Dads were recruited as Saturday morning teachers – at the convent – on Quimby Avenue for struggling young students.

Sighting nursing nuns wearing bright white habits sailing along Hough's dusty streets became commonplace!

Following and caring were those faithful moms who had picked their one-day-a-week to volunteer and never missed their assigned day.

Jane and a neighbor, Isabelle Coleman, can attest to that!

The day the Hough riots began was a Wednesday – Jane's day to volunteer.

With Isabelle, they found machine guns mounted on Jeeps stationed on every street corner in Hough, and they were shouted back home by outraged National Guardsmen trying to keep white women volunteers out of a black war zone!

Jane and son, Tim, were seen painting and repairing until our Quimby Avenue new friends were getting along better, but our friendship with Fr. Albert had two more adventures!

First, Jane was determined to help Fr. Albert "rid the area of rats" (quoted from the article in the <u>Plain Dealer</u> that first grabbed her attention).

Fr. Albert's idea prevailed by his insisting that an exterminating company be engaged – with auxiliary funds – when Jane wished to provide her own poison!

Our second adventure was far and away an impossible happening!

It *was* far and away – in Mexico City!

Jane and husband, Harry, had joined Jane's brother, Jimmy Sutphin, and his wife, Louise, in going to the summer Olympic Games in 1968, held in Mexico City.

Summer Olympic Games had been an Al Sutphin family tradition since the Los Angeles games in 1932 – followed by London, England; Helsinki, Finland; and Rome, Italy, in 1960.

As the two couples were wandering the stadium sites – to locate the venue of the track and field events planned for the next day – Fr. Albert appeared, out of nowhere!

Fr. Albert, Fr. Albert – how could this be happening?

Jane was excited. She knew that Fr. Albert's Spanish was – of course – fluent, and she had been taking private lessons to prepare her for Mexico City.

She will practice on Fr. Albert!

Jane immediately introduces her brother as, "mi hermoso." They continue on for the entire day of sight-seeing, with Fr. Albert in tow.

As the day draws to a close, Fr. Albert asks Jane why she has spent the entire day telling everyone, "She is beautiful." Jane has confused "hermano" (brother) with "hermoso" (beautiful).

They laugh for the rest of the week!

## LESSON: TEN SPANISH LESSONS DO NOT A LINGUIST MAKE!

Harry Leitch escapes!

Harry is a Spotter for the Cleveland Browns on Sundays, with Jim Graner, commentator on radio.

That Sunday, the Browns are playing the Baltimore Colts in Baltimore, and the Browns are in a slump.

Harry is known as their No. 1 cheerleader!

When he leaves Mexico City for Baltimore, he arrives wearing a three-foot wide, gold-decorated Mexican Sombrero to cheer everyone on to victory.

Harry can barely be seen under the hat!

The Browns lose 34 – 0!

(Please remember the earlier, 1964 Championship game (our last win): Browns, 27 – Baltimore, 0!)

The Sutphins' growing family is pondering an enormous "Family Proposal," dreamed about by their Dad – now called "The Champ" by his sons-in-law, who can't beat him at the family ritual, 500 rummy!

The Champ announces that whatever money his estate now has will be spent on an eighteen-member Sutphin family trip to Europe in July of 1964.

He has something – a momentous event – from WWI and the trenches in France that he must share with all the family he loves!

It involves Battery D and his war comrades and an old mill located in Neuville, France. We will stand on a bridge overlooking the old mill!

The Sutphin married daughters, Jane, Carolyn and Alberta, now have seventeen children under thirteen; and their brother, Jimmy, and Louise have three, making twenty (ten boys and ten girls) – forming the Sutphin picture of the future!

Al Sutphin can't wait any longer. He is seventy years old.

Hold on!

Baby brother, Cal, wishes to be heard!

He is a salesman for Braden Sutphin in the family tradition, having started in the shipping room in high school and now on the road in the Baltimore-Washington, D.C. territory.

He is 24 years old – 1963 is the year. Cal has been calling on Globe Poster, a favorite printer friend of his brother, Jimmy, when he called on owner, Norman Shapiro.

Now, Cal calls on Lee Zimmerman (married to Bernice Shapiro), and Cal's life takes a huge "right turn!"

Her name is Sandra DiAngelo. She is the eighteen-year-old, charming receptionist for Globe Poster.

Everyone loves her at Globe, so when a Braden Sutphin Ink salesman – from Cleveland, Ohio – becomes interested, the Zimmermans are encouraging "love in bloom!"

Sandy describes her early years as those of the oldest of five, and from very humble circumstances in a loving, Italian family. Her two grandmothers live on either side, and – in the Italian tradition – help rear, nurture, and perform all family duties as *one* big family together.

Her Dad, Sam, is a conductor on a Baltimore – New York City run that gives Sandy dreams of living in the Big Apple someday.

Her mother, Mary, is part German – with a delightful sense of humor and fun to know – always telling it like it is!

Sandy's only brother, John, becomes a Braden Sutphin salesman – then becomes a world traveler with a German manufacturer of huge printing presses!

Jeanette, Mary Beth, and Cindy have children. We all enjoy family celebrations, but not often enough, as we live many miles apart!

Sandy had led her younger siblings to look to the future, as Sandy accepted her first after-high-school employment, as a receptionist.

What followed was an unannounced engagement – at eighteen – to an unknown, out-of-town salesman, Cal Sutphin, who was not being considered as anyone worthy of their cherished oldest daughter, just entering her adult years!

Even with Braden Sutphin Ink headquarters ensconced now for sixty years in Cleveland, Ohio, Cal was imagining a branch of his own in Baltimore – near Sandy's family.

The girls, Jane, Carolyn, and Alberta, all questioned the wisdom of leaving their seventeen children motherless and fatherless for seven weeks – while being thousands of miles overseas!

Our mother was instructed that her job would be "head honcho" at home, with grandfather Gaga Sutphin as solo parents to twenty children under thirteen.

Gaga Sutphin voiced his opinion: Albert has gone too far this time!"

Our mother started month-long novenas. Our much-experienced (decade-long) *sitters* began counting their money in 1964 dollars.

Cal and Sandy had a big decision to make. Their wedding, which had been planned for September, was then moved up to the July 11th weekend in 1964.

"The Trip" was planned for a Queen Elizabeth sailing on July 16.

We would all spend the wedding weekend in Baltimore with the rehearsal dinner on Friday night, the 10th, at a charming old Candlelight Lodge, with a Catholic Mass following at noon on Saturday, July 11.

At the last minute, Sandy had closed her bank account on Friday before the bank closed at 2 p.m. She will be living in Cleveland, Ohio. To her horror, she receives a call from her future father-in-law to come to his hotel; he has a check for her made out in her maiden name. She must cash it before her name changes tomorrow!

It is 4 p.m. She rushes to her bank, which closed at 2 p.m. She cries and knocks and knocks and cries. They cash the check!

Sandy has passed her first test as a Sutphin outlaw.

Cal and Sandy have made their decision. They will spend their honeymoon with eighteen members of this overwhelming family!

Since the sailing is not until July 16, Cal and Sandy have almost a week to hide in New York City – in order to spend their first married days alone – and avoid the eighteen members of the family, who are staying at the Abbey Hotel at West 51st and Seventh Avenue.

They find their own hotel!

Alone at last!

Oops! They run into ten family members at the theatre district at Times Square.

They beg for privacy! All those new in-laws grant it! No one tells!

Those in-laws have been having the time of their lives at the New York World's Fair! What's not to like! Astonishing new electronics – cell phones – TV cable access – early business hook-ups – all draw world-wide attention and enlighten us (55 years ago!).

July 16, 1964, finds us all together at Pier 91, the Cunard Line main dock. We are destined for the Mezzanine deck – first class, not way up on top – but our version of heaven!

We are so excited, we might as well have been sailing as the Captain's Preferred Passengers.

Cal and Sandy are finally "among us" and have a big surprise awaiting them as their first inkling at the Sutphin sense of fun.

Their big, beautiful stateroom has many handsome amenities, but *no beds*! Even though ordinarily bolted to the floor (deck), Al Sutphin had had them removed for the first night (only).

Sandy thought this might be punishment for Cal and her opting out in New York City the night Paul and Katy Brown were entertaining the entire wedding party – and they had stood everyone up! (It wasn't!)

The duo of Harry and Jane paid an even bigger price. It involved the entire five-day voyage to Cherbourg, on board their first-ever cruise! (They had never had the time or money for a honeymoon trip in 1950.

Harry's snoring had caused separate rooms at home.

Al Sutphin found this an ideal chance to save money – eliminating an entire stateroom and the expense involved!

Harry would sleep with his father-in-law, and Jane would sleep with her single sister, Mary E.!

All went well – until the third day aboard. Jane and Mary E.'s stateroom had a door leading to Jimmy and Louise's quarters.

Jane suggested that Mary E. attend the movie on board for the entire afternoon, and announced to brother, Jimmy, and Louise that her stateroom would be off limits to everyone – except *Harry* – for the afternoon.

The lovers were nude and happily engaged when there was much banging and calling through the door by their steward.

Horrified, the lovers locked themselves in the "head" (Harry had been in the Navy), when the steward broke in!

He was stunned! He had been alerted by Louise Sutphin that something must be amiss; her sisters-in-law had never locked their door – ever!

When next the lovers encountered Louise in the dining salon that evening, she could only blush and reply, "I forgot!"

Harry, meanwhile, had discovered that drinking with his brother, Bob (Carolyn's husband), till four or five a.m. every night found him entering his father-in-law's stateroom every morning about 6 a.m. His father-in-law was just getting up, adjusting his green eye-shade to start answering the mail – all lights on!

Harry had nowhere to sleep. The Champ was up for the day!

(Harry was known to sleep alone in Mary E. and Jane's bathtub during the day.)

Jane always wondered, when the stewards were all furloughed in Cherbourg, how the conversations went about "that Sutphin family" from Cleveland, Ohio!

The Champ arrived the happiest of men! He had crossed to Cherbourg now for the sixth decade – beginning in WWI in 1918, his honeymoon in 1922, and now with twenty beloved grandchildren safely at home with his wife and father looking after his "Gang." He was about to have his 22$^{nd}$ visit with Pierre Gillot and his family in Pierrefitte at the Café du Commerce.

The Calvados is waiting! Eighteen Americans are very thirsty! (Spanish Calvados is now on sale at Heinen's in 2015.)

Ramone, our bus driver, is about to experience the most informed travel guide of his long career with Americans – The Champ, who is occupying the tour guide seat up front.

We renew this friendship with all the Cunard personnel who had greeted the four single Sutphin daughters in 1949. Now, they are watching us embark – but on a new odyssey – to see the WWII beach landings of D-Day, 1944!

Ray Stoney and Bob Leitch were with General Patton's Third Army. They were not in D-Day on the beaches, but later at Bastogne in Belgium.

However, the Visitor Centers at Utah Beach (the Americans) and Juno (the British beachhead) still mesmerized us with the maps and routes of all the converging forces and, sadly, the nearby resting places for the boys who were there, forever enshrined!

We hardly spoke back on the bus!

It was understood – from our wild night in Cherbourg – that every morning, the bus would be boarded by six a.m. – everybody aboard!

"The Honeymooners" were never late, because the very first morning in Cherbourg, they settled in the first double seat – just inside the door – and never relinquished it for all seven weeks.

They were first on and first off to their room – wherever it was – and during the day, on the bus, they opened huge maps of Europe, behind which they hid themselves – and no wonder!

What was happening – in the back of the bus – during "Happy Hour" was a practiced scenario!

Ramone was instructed (by The Champ) to find a Shoppe selling Spirits and all "wines of the region," and stop there!

The back door of the bus would then fly open, and the "designators of the day," with enough Francs, would rush out and return "loaded for bear." The laughing soon took over!

At Pierrefitte, since The Champ had given Ramone perfect directions, the entire Gillot family awaited us.

We have pictures of emerging – after a very "wet" lunch – with all the husbands carrying their wives, except Jane, who is carrying Harry.

As reported earlier, we have been on a mission!

Included in our eighteen family members are two couples – the wives of whom are thought of as our adopted sisters.

Odette lives near Metz and was employed at the banking establishment where our Dad did all his banking for 30-odd years. Odette, after the war, married Roger, who had been captured with his father by the Nazis and forced to work in a German munitions plant until liberated by the American forces!

She and Roger accompanied us to Paris for two weeks.

Lucille Garber had been an "adopted" sister from Ashland, Ohio, and a much-loved daughter of Ora and Edna Garber, long-time "inseparable link" of Al Sutphin and the Braden Sutphin Ink Company.

Lucille was now married to Larry Ford, who was running the A. L. Garber Printing Company in Ashland, Ohio.

She was studying for her PhD (as Provost of Ashland College) in the 1960s. A requirement for PhD accreditation was a PhD in French!

Her linguistic abilities will save our mission – in a little while – in this story! And so will her camera.

She and Larry joined us in Cherbourg by plane, as Lucille had to take her exams the day we sailed from New York.

After our visit to acquaint so many new Sutphins with the Gillot family, we are in Metz for the night.

The Champ has been stressing the utter importance of enough film for our day of days, the mission to the "Old Mill" in Neuville.

None of us have heard the Champ's story, but brother Jimmy is horrified to find his camera out of order and out of film.

He and Louise confide in Lucille. (Louise has been looking for film at every stop.)

Lucille's camera is a new, hi-tech, American-style camera that uses canisters – not film.

Louise borrows Lucille's camera and rushes to the main street in Metz – just before the day's long drive to Neuville, France, where the "Old Mill" family tour awaits Champ's story.

As the bus is ready to leave, Louise rushes on board – flashing the canisters that she has found – and considers that a major miracle has taken place.

The camera shop was "old world." How did a dusty little shop with a beaded doorway and nothing modern to display have the hi-tech canisters?

Jimmy and Louise know that, halfway to Neuville (150 miles), is Navarre, France, where St. Bernadette is buried. They plan a stop and make a promise. They will visit St. Bernadette's burial site and promise that if they have another child, they will name her "Bernadette."

(Six years later, in 1970, on March 18, Susan *Bernadette* is born – Jimmy and Louise's promised daughter and, miraculously, a girl!)

St. Bernadette is a favorite saint of our mother, because of so many miracles performed at "her" founding holy place, Lourdes.

She also is buried in a glass coffin, with seemingly perfectly preserved hands and face. (A note confirms that her hands and face have been waxed for preservation.)

After a very long 300-mile day, we arrive in Neuville, knowing that tomorrow is our day on a very ancient bridge, overlooking an old mill. It is the moment Albert Claude Sutphin has promised himself – since he was eighteen years old. He would return someday and share with his family – if he's lucky – what WWI at this place meant to him!

As we line up – all eighteen of us – across the arched span of a very ancient bridge, we are seeing a working mill with centuries of worn stones still intact.

As water tumbles from the ancient wheel, the ladies of the village are on their hands and knees scrubbing their laundry against the flat rocks and enjoying their labors and one another's company.

None of us were even "a thought" when last Al Sutphin faced what he saw as the "last hours of his life!"

His Battery D of the aforementioned 135th Field Artillery had been together since their neighborhood school days in Cleveland. As life-long friends and relatives, they had signed up together – to go to war!

In Montgomery, Alabama, they were prepared for war as a team – fighting as a unit – being taught to protect one another. (Today, we say, "having your back!") They were *safe* as long as they were together!

On their second night at the mill, after a long ocean voyage had successfully dodged German U-Boats, they are mentally preparing themselves for "The Front" – only several miles away.

They can hear the guns!

Al Sutphin feels a sharp blow to the bottoms of his feet. It is two a.m.!

His commanding officer announces, "Sutphin, you are going to 'The Front' *by yourself.* There is an ox cart waiting to take you there alone. Good luck!"

In all the intervening years, Champ had never been able to understand the hatred this commander held for him – or why!

He never mentioned his name, and it took years to recover from believing that that ox cart ride was his last hour on earth!

Jimmy has recorded the story, and the hour-long canister picture has captured the scene!

We say nothing on the ride to Verdun, where we will spend the night overlooking another battlefield and knowing that three million young boys had died there – now a peaceful summer meadow – no hint of the hell war had wrought in 1918.

After touring Champ's favorite French countryside, we arrive in Tours, the famous Chateau region of French kings- especially Francis the First, whose huge entourages numbered 500 attendants and hundreds of carriages- to transport his household for just a week or two!

We enjoyed a fabulous luncheon out-of-doors on a sunlit terrace, where Larry Ford found himself with three martinis served all at once!

He was confused – as he had ordered only *one*!

We solved his dilemma. He ordered one *dry* martini. Our waiter spoke German! Ein, zwei, drei – one, two, *three*! A *drei* martini meant *three*!

Champ had loved Paris during days of R & R after the Armistice – November 11, 1918 – and before returning home!

His best buddies, Bill Reiser, Al Betz, and brother-in-law, Dan Hoynes, had all survived the war and found new ways to celebrate victory in night-time Paris.

The Lutetia Hotel on the Left Bank was our headquarters and an old home to Al Sutphin's 20-some trips to Paris!

We could walk to the Luxembourg Gardens and our favorite "Bon Marche" for shopping.

Harry and Bob, after taking Jane and Carolyn to the famous Les Hall Market at 4:30 a.m., left for home – and back to work – leaving Mary E. to share a triple bedroom for the rest of the trip and a stateroom on the Queen Mary with three bunks also for Jane and Carolyn.

After Paris, we headed to Spain with stops all along the way.

Neuchatel, Switzerland, was a one and only group shopping event – enjoyed by gift-starved shoppers. We leaped off the bus as though shot out of a cannon!

Champ was allowing the only two-hour mass buying spree of the entire trip!

Our "take home" purchases were displayed that evening in a private dining room in our hotel!

It was Christmas in July, marked by envy and laughter.

Not any two of us had found the same gifts, prompting our favorite question: "I love that – how much do you want for it?"

As we headed for Spain and a new language, we reflected on the two languages we were leaving behind – French and German.

Can their differences ever be resolved – except by armed combat? There have been the Franco-Prussian war and WWI and WWII conflicts.

Take for instance, "whipped cream." In French, it's "avec crème." In German, "mit schlag." Reconciliation, "avec schlag?" It doesn't sound likely.

We did have an immediate language challenge in Madrid, Spain.

In a local Farmacia, we tried to explain the ravages of our daily dose in Paris of mozzarella cheese on French onion soup. Only *sign* language purchased our much-needed Preparation H!

At the Prado Museum, El Greco and his black velvet paintings were amazing.

At the Alhambra, Moorish conquerors made tiles of 1,000 artisans – mind-boggling!

The departure from Cherbourg on the Queen Mary re-introduced us to our old-fashioned wardrobe trunks, with our very formal attire and our dear old pals – the very faithful stewards, who greeted us like long-lost friends!

Back at home, our sitters are thrilled to see us – for twenty reasons – the children! They have survived, and they will rush to their banks the very next day.

Jane and Harry had a whole family sitting for their six children: The Kopps. They soon cashed their check, and sent a son to college!

Unhappily, Jane and Harry found their eleven-year-old daughter, Mary, smoking – with their sitters' permission. End of friendship!

Happily, on to the Schodt family, who lived on our Corydon Road in St. Ann's parish!

Matt and Schottie – from Norway – had included Dorothy, Schottie's sister, in their threesome.

Between them all, Jane and Harry's children had the best care ever!

The Schodt threesome loved three-year-old Hal. They called him "our little blond Halie!" They regularly made him his favorite "red yellow" (Jello) dessert.

Hal grew up never forgetting their love and kindness to him.

Married to Barbara Vetsos, they named their second son, Matt – in honor of Matt Schodt – and visited them in Matt Schodt's retirement home in Holiday, Florida, many times (until their deaths).

A year after our return, Gaga Sutphin died on the Farm in Ft. Myers, Florida. Sutton and Gramma Hoynes had died a decade before.

Michael and Gramma Hoynes are buried with his large Irish family in Calvary Cemetery at E. 130th and Miles.

Gaga and Sutton are buried (now with our parents) in Colonial Gardens on Colonial Blvd. in Ft. Myers.

Gaga's sisters and two husbands are also buried there, making it a Sutphin family circle.

Our mother had her plot blessed by a favorite Catholic priest in 1985.

Gaga is our only nonagenarian – 93 years old in 1965.

We hoped that the fatherless and motherless grandchildren – the year before – weren't too much for him!

He is sorely missed!

In 1967, Albert Sutphin retired from Braden Sutphin Ink Company and remained in Ft. Myers, leaving Jimmy and Cal in charge at 3650 E. 93rd Street, Cleveland, Ohio, headquarters.

After a stroke, Al doesn't want to be seen in a wheelchair in his beloved hometown!

He is in touch every day with his company and his Cleveland connections.

He writes thousands of letters, and with his mind intact, has lots of ideas on how to run everything – from ink – to sports – to grandchildren (now counting 28), with The Honeymooners soon to contribute seven, all together!

With Ft. Myers a permanent resting place for the original "head of family," it might be an auspicious moment to describe the Braden Sutphin Farm on the Caloosahatchee River ("Calm River") on Sutphin Place in Ft. Myers, Florida.

In the late 1930s, Florida was a very depressed real estate market – having no hope of attracting second-home winter buyers. Al Sutphin has tried three winters in central Florida – DeLeon Springs – where the children loved a defunct hotel area and a very large cement pool and fishing stream to catch bluegills – for the very first time. However, some days, their Cleveland snow suits were better gear than bathing suits.

Enter Al Sutphin's uncle Will Clark (mentioned earlier). He had married Gaga's sister, and they were very happily ensconced in a much warmer Ft. Myers, where winters were warmer and sunnier!

It also carried the mystique of the remarkable inventor, Thomas Alva Edison, whose home and laboratory on the Caloosahatchee was a celebrated tourist attraction!

Albert came looking!

Al and Mary are intrigued by an abandoned stretch of 2,000-front footage on the river – now a matted jungle – for $5.00 a front foot!

Forty thousand dollars will buy 40 acres of pines and palms, connected by Tarzan-like ropes of jungle vines. There is a moccasin snake in a muddy creek, an alligator slithering around, and three sadly-in-need-of-paint wooden structures.

One was a make-shift barn, turned home, when the elegant main house burned to the ground. It had six bedrooms, four baths, and a large dining/kitchen area. Perfect for guests!

The second was a four-room, wooden, nautical-type house with the only entrance a gangplank (as on a boat)! Perfect for Al and Mary.

The third was a cabana-type, men and women's bathhouse – overlooking and trapped in jungle greenery – a badly damaged swimming pool! Perfect for meandering raccoons!

It was a former Miles Laboratory property, left to three Miles sons – 2,000 feet each. The son/owner of these 40 acres had long since given up interest of ownership.

It took thirty months to clear the Tarzan-like jungle, remove the deadly moccasin, build a roomy cage for the alligator – now named "Chuckles" – and start planting every imaginable flowering tree and citrus orchard grove of oranges, grapefruit, and mangoes – some for turpentine, some for desserts.

A half-mile-long Australian pine road ran the length of the property, and a beautiful barn with a clamshell drive now dominated the south side.

The glory of purple and orange jacarandas glowed every May, and geraniums grew in white cement planters facing the river for all 2,000 feet!

Homes grew too! (Seven in all.)

Facing the river now were simple, single-story white houses, with blue tile roofs and red doors and shutters – Al Sutphin's red, white and blue blossoms one more time!

Every house had a fireplace and a mirror that reflected the river indoors.

As the guest list grew, Braden Sutphin salesmen retired, and printing friends came with winter sport figures, like Paul and Katy Brown, Bill and Mary Ellen Summers, Whitey Lewis, and Ice Follies owners Shipstad & Johnson, so grew the accommodations!

Now, a big new apartment complex with four units with picture windows dominated the northern side, and seven row apartments along the river's south side with *indoor* showers (after years of early morning bathing out-of-doors).

Guests loved it!

This description now introduces the 70s – when Al and Mary Sutphin celebrate their 50th anniversary on that Braden Sutphin-style Ft. Myers Farm!

Please join us!

## CHAPTER VI

# THE 1970S

The 50th anniversary of Albert and Mary Hoynes Sutphin was celebrated with their 28 grandchildren and many family friends in Ft. Myers, Florida, on their Braden Sutphin Farm. It was August 22, 1972.

The 27-hour bus ride for 44 members of the party – Cleveland to Ft. Myers – was a challenge in itself.

No one realized that bus drivers must be relieved every four union hours, and therefore must change drivers at the downtown bus terminal for every exchange.

The bus terminals are sometimes twenty miles off the State and Federal highways – sometimes necessitating one-and-a-half-hour exchanges.

All we passengers found snacks and then jogged around before reboarding.

By late the second day, our 1,600-mile trip – by bus – was a bad idea!

Those who played cards and sipped – a lot – had become loud and rowdy, to the complete annoyance of those trying to talk or sleep.

Meanwhile, at the scene of the celebrations, frantic decorating ideas are in play.

Our sisters, Carolyn and Alberta, had already flown to the Farm five days ahead of the bus' arrival.

They had already planned the sleeping arrangements for all 44 members arriving by bus.

Carolyn and Alberta had also been transforming the "Casino" dining room into a garden bower, using live green ivy taken from the outside walls of Carolyn and Bob Leitch's house in Westlake, Ohio. The ivy had been packed in boxes with wet newspapers to carry on the plane!

After removing thirty years of family pictures, mirrors and keepsakes from the Casino walls, they apply damp ivy from ceiling to floor around the entire room.

An arbor had been placed at the entrance, borrowed from one of the seventeen housing units on the Farm.

The 40 acres have been transformed with extra flower boxes all along the 2,000-foot frontage on the Caloosahatchee River.

The shuffleboard court, newly marked, and all red chairs (from the now "Old Cleveland Arena") had been painted!

A fountain now bubbled away in a corner of the dining area, setting the tone for a garden party indoors.

The bus arrives!

Weary and beleaguered family members are immediately refreshed by the sight of the Farm at its beautiful best!

The sleeping arrangements have housed all grandsons – sixteen and older – in the large new barn dormitory.

The Leitch sisters, Carolyn and Jane, together have four sons over sixteen, and two fifteen-year-olds who plead not be housed with their very young boy cousins.

Ray and Alberta Stoney have twin boys, Ray, Jr., and Matt, over sixteen.

The big boys accept the fifteen-year-olds as long as they agree to be their "gofers" (called slaves!).

The new barn is now dormitory to ten rioting, 24-hour, wild hooligans!

The little boys are housed in a guest house closer to parents.

All the girls, big and little, are having a wonderful time in the "the Annex" – a guest house with three bathrooms.

Altogether, 28 are running around for the next week – never to be tamed!

The main event of the memorable week is the dinner in the garden-style casino.

The Champ loves violin music!

Not *one* violin, but *many* violins!!

The Ft. Myers Symphony Orchestra supplies six well-rehearsed violinists.

Their conductor has been firmly instructed that his players must have mastered the great tunes of Paris in the 20s – Al and Mary's honeymoon year.

We would love to have Ernest Hemingway and the Fitzgeralds join our family that special evening.

Who wouldn't?

Seating is tight!

The Champ has refused to hold this very personal event anywhere but at "The Farm." (No impersonal ballroom or restaurant downtown.)

The Casino was the largest building, but seventy diners was max.

On this occasion, seating had to be found for 105!

Mary, the 76-year-old bride, rushed around the jammed dining room – seating the rambunctious grandchildren, folding napkins, arranging place cards, greeting early guests – busy, busy, everywhere!

Albert, the 78-year-old groom, sits quietly disengaged.

Suddenly, he stands up, taps his water glass for everyone's attention, and announces:

"As you can see, I have obviously taken better care of Mary than she has of me!"

Everyone loved it. It was the real Al Sutphin!

Carolyn and Alberta were the master sardine-makers! People who barely knew one another became fast friends!

Jane needed entrance space, as well, for the "Show" that she had been writing for months.

Now the rehearsals – all parts played by the grandchildren – were being performed in the "Big House" (six bedrooms, four baths).

(On the original Dr. Miles homestead, this was the location of his mansion. When a fire reduced it to rubble, Dr. Miles moved a huge barn from the back of the property and installed it on the site of the former mansion.

Now, the Barn was the main guest house, and held the prime view of the river.

Jane's show was running too long for people jammed into tight quarters. Jane, being a Theatre/English major from Flora Stone Mather, Western Reserve University class of '47, saw no problem! She would talk fast!

The opening number set the tone!

It featured four of the oldest and biggest grandsons.

They were costumed in authentic WWI Army Expeditionary Force uniforms with the famous tin helmets and were singing "The Mademoiselle from Armentieres – Parlez-vous!"

The show covered highlights of their lives, including Olympic Games of Helsinki, Finland, with Jimmy and Cal. Now, their grandsons were dressed in track and field outfits of the summer games.

Every aspect of the show had authentic costumes and was narrated by a fast-talking Jane.

Sometimes, the actors couldn't keep up with the many costume changes – especially the ukulele chorus depicting their dating years. Jane had to resort to 1920s (with six ukuleles and strummers)! Jane's humor when marking time for costume changes:

George Burns asks Gracie, "What do you think of Red China, Gracie?"

Gracie answers, "I like it on a yellow table cloth!"

The sweltering diners laugh!

Jane is relieved!

Albert saves the evening by announcing his surprise for his bride – fireworks over the river.

Everyone rushes outside and finds that -- even with August humidity – it's cooler!

To the grandchildren, the father and son baseball game at a real stadium, Terry Park, in East Ft. Myers, was the lifetime event.

The girl grandchildren, unanimously wearing real vendor outfits, sell popcorn and peanuts from real stadium trays and cold pop from ice chests.

The boys and Dads wear big-league baseball uniforms – the balls, bats, and gloves are regulation. Harry and Jane's son, Hal Leitch, was the catcher and drove in the winning run, making the sons the winner of the father/son trophy Champ provided.

Carolyn Sutphin Leitch was the designated scorekeeper – who did all things right – when it came to math!

Champ was proud – really proud!!

Back at the Farm, the winners – our young Lochinvars, as Champ called them – did some underage beer guzzling and threw Aunt Bertie Stoney into the pool.

Later, in the Casino – in her wet clothes – the air conditioner caused a cold that lasted for three weeks, keeping her from ever forgetting the anniversary week or those bad boys – *her sister's sons* who threw her into the pool. (Not *her* boys, surely?)

There actually is a huge "thank you" always owed to Aunt Bertie.

She serves on every committee before and stays after for clean-up. Her forte!

Alberta and husband, Ray Stoney, moved to the Braden Sutphin Farm in 1952 to become managers.

They brought baby Gail – one year old – and added identical twin brothers, Ray, Jr., and Matt, then three more sisters, Ann, Lynn and Elaine, in the next twelve Ft. Myer years.

When they returned, it was not to Cleveland! They travelled on to Detroit, where they opened the first Braden Sutphin branch in 1963.

The story of the 50$^{th}$ anniversary is a microcosm of their twelve years of guests to manage, poem nights to arrange and 45 acres to be kept beautiful, palm fronds fallen and to be collected every day, grass to be cut, houses to be painted, and a million little things to be fixed.

All this was co-handled with the expertise of Jack Gibson, who followed after Ray, and managed for the next thirty years, with a staff of only four or five helpers!

From 1940 to 1973, our mother and father dressed as London music hall entertainers "Gallagher and Shean" and delivered their own version of the Gallagher-Shean routine (involving the names of their guests that week), and Poem Night was a sensation – as were the original poems (executed by the guests) after a few self-conscious moments!

Albert and Mary Hoynes Sutphin were creators of wonderful things – driven by a love of sharing with others.

Their Cleveland Arena brought hope to a Depression-ravaged city. Thousands found work and a new life because Al Sutphin borrowed $1,000,000 – on his signature – and paid it all back with interest.

## LESSON: LOVE YOUR HOMETOWN!

The Braden Sutphin Farm – reclaimed from a jungle – (six miles from downtown Ft. Myers) ignited real estate sales in an abandoned area where there were no shops, and the streets nearby were unpaved.

The Depression was still on when the Sutphins arrived in Fort Myers and saw enormous possibilities, if you worked hard and cared enough!

Jake Mohler, father of ten children, became the early builder of Al Sutphin's dream homes – simple one-story and easy to manage (not one lost a roof in the 1960 hurricane, Donna).

Al Sutphin drew all his house plans for Jake in the sand with his cane!

Many of the now-successful guests had had the same humble beginning as did Al and Mary Sutphin.

Some still loved the natural beauty and humble accommodations of wooden one-story buildings – shower outside and Al and Mary's poem nights – where the guests worried all week about *that poem they had to write*!

They may have now afforded designer clothes, but their best duds left (after ten days) with a brand-new, hand-sewn label, "This article was stolen from the Braden Sutphin Farm."

When this very original husband, father, and friend died on June 25, 1974, just two years after their 50th anniversary, daughter-in-law, Sandy DiAngelo Sutphin wrote (and I quote):

"To have a father-in-law who used his powers for good – who took care of his family and a whole city – is a special blessing for all of us!"

"He reared children with a work ethic that allowed them to be successful in every way."

"More importantly, he impressed them to give back!"

"He did many wonderful things that made a difference in many lives."

"This family has the biggest heart, made possible by the one who was also the heart and soul of their family – their loving mother!"

## LESSON: WHOEVER HAS A HEART FULL OF LOVE, ALWAYS HAS SOMETHING TO GIVE! – POPE JOHN XXIII.

Our mother, Mary, lived on in the special house Champ had designed for her.

It was H-shaped – the crossover between two suites was a walkway from Mary's side – all antiques collected on trips with Albert – to *his side*, ultra-modern – all chrome and red leather – with his Edison Dictaphone close at hand and plenty of ashtrays for those El Verso cigars!

The permanent guests – now renting – were mainly widows of Albert's salesmen, and had become Mary's best friends – all enjoying dinners out and Lawrence Welk together on Saturday nights at 7:00 p.m. on "Mary's side!"

Property taxes were now $30,000 a year, grass cutting $1,000 in the growing season, and minimum maintenance for 40 acres was more than seemed possible any longer!

In the late 70s, it became increasingly clear that some kind of "income property" needed to be created.

The "Look of Genesis" was born!

Years of exercise classes in Cleveland led Jane to think "Spa" for that beautiful tropical paradise in Ft. Myers.

When brother, Jimmy, offered financial backing from Braden Sutphin Ink, it became a fait accompli.

Jack Gibson, now Farm manager, relished the idea of using his carpenter skills – long neglected – to turn the south-side Barn (next to an orange grove) into men and women's massage and a beauty salon.

A tennis court was added, and a sauna and hot tub were placed nearby, where fragrant orange blossoms would waft and please the guests sunning outside in the tub!

Our mother was now hostess to Spa enthusiasts – and given a whole new lease on life.

She also was matriarch of four generations – now in charge of the whole operation!

Jane, daughter Mary Dana, and her own Heather, four years old now, were the original "staffers."

Jane recruited well-known YMCA expert, Dorothy Stenger, as boss. Dorothy, at 70, was a role model for every health-conscious visitor who followed her from Cleveland.

Dorothy brought her "gals."

Helen Godman, a diet expert, offered to train Mary Dana on how to make 900-calorie meals a day simply delicious; Helen would then retire. (She was married, and lived on Cape Coral, across the river.)

Katie Pappas was jack-of-all-trades – cook, exercise expert, and wonderful to have around.

She did the high-calorie cooking nightly in the staff house – to everyone's delight – after a long, exhausting day!

Alan Krueger took early retirement from The Cleveland Athletic Club and was in charge of all pool exercises!

One visitor – scared to death of water – actually learned to swim lengths of the pool in one week.

Did Jane mention that Alan was very good looking?

Edie, young and trained in ballet, was in charge of late afternoon yoga – on red leather mats out by the river!

Our day began with a mile walk – sheltered by the Australian pines – along the length of the property!

Following a cleansing swallow of saffron oil, honey and vinegar in a shot glass, there was a quiet hour in your comfortable quarters before morning exercises – led by Dorothy – in the Casino!

Swimming exercises followed (after a break, and juice or broth was served).

Lunch was next, and then two hours of quiet time. Meditation on the deck, overlooking the river, was popular. So was reading – books were available in the Casino library or quietly in your room.

Magdalena, 72, the Spa masseuse, was at attention in the Barn! So was Sylvia in the beauty salon for facials or hairdos, with her assistant, Gloria.

Dinner gave our mother a chance to enjoy the guests and they to enjoy her – where all four generations gathered every night and presented a united family, happy at their tasks!

LESSON: COMMON GOALS – A FAMILY MAKE!

Evenings offered the guests either Dorothy at the organ (a gift of Paul and Katie Brown) or Edie creating an original ballet. Alan Krueger gave a clarinet recital until the instrument broke into 2 sections, and guest, Bill Boehm, remarked, "Alan plays only in half notes!"

Some evenings featured "psychic" professionals, who lectured on "putting life in order!" There were also some health and nutrition experts who gave hints to live by – and pamphlets to take home.

## LESSON: FOCUS ON YOUR *INNER CHILD*, WHO NEEDS PROTECTION, NURTURING AND, ABOVE ALL, KINDNESS.

We had old friends from California one week.

Diana Nagler, married to Gern Nagler (now retired from his years with the Cleveland Browns), were almond farmers in Sacramento, California.

Diana's best girlfriends – making four for the week – loved Florida's warm winter nights (California has cold evenings) and everything about the Spa.

They were coming back next year.

Old college friend from Western Reserve University, Bill Boehm, of the Singing Angels, came for one week – lost seven pounds and stayed for a second week – and lost fourteen pounds altogether!

Bill Wilhelm brought "Mrs." Wilhelm. We knew immediately that they weren't married – they were having such a good time!

Bill and Dody became wonderful forever friends!

Bill returned the very next week with his darling daughter, Mary (then seventeen), and promised to bring everyone he knew from Cleveland next year.

Next year never happened!

We were left with fabulous memories of Bill Wilhelm on his departure with Dody, raving about how much better he felt – and clutching his bulging briefcase.

As he got to his car, the briefcase dropped, and a dozen Hershey candy bars – with almonds – fell out onto the driveway.

Heaven only knows how many he had arrived with!

## LESSON: MORE EMPHASIS NEEDED ON FRUITS AND VEGETABLES.

We were invited to their wedding a year later, where Mary Dana and Jane told the story of the Wilhelm Spa adventure – and everybody loved it!

The economics of the early 80s did us no favors.

Jimmy was running Braden Sutphin Ink and was our brave benefactor.

When a recession made it impossible to hold out for the years it would take the Spa to pay for itself and then make a profit, he had to think again!

Jimmy's thoughts ran to the constant pleas of The Landings – next door on the river – to sell any riverfront frontage we could spare.

It seemed, with Champ gone and those remarkable days over, we could sell 1,200 feet of waterfront and keep 800 feet (twelve acres) for our family and, in particular, our mother's home!

The Landings now were directly adjacent to our own waterfront, and they immediately began the construction of eight riverfront homes and a large marina to serve those new owners.

It was called Riverside.

Our Spa was now half of The Landings' new waterfront. We cried!

Jane felt that it had been the younger Sutphins' finest hour – even though nothing would ever equal what our amazing parents had achieved in their forty years and their thousands of guests with splendid memories of paradise – Al and Mary style!

Memories of Bill Summers, American League umpire, and Mary Ellen. Bill played Pope John Paul in a skit!

Paul Brown (and Katie) who, with the Summers, spent twenty winters, and who played Emperor Hirohito in a skit!

A test of the trusted friendship of Al and Mary – with Paul Brown – happened early in the 60s when Paul was let go by Art Modell.

The media had descended on the Browns' residence, and they escaped to Jane and Harry's house on Corydon Road in Cleveland Heights – at Paul's request!

Paul was shattered! Nothing in his amazing career prepared him for dismissal!

Our Dad – ever the business executive – counseled Paul, "If you ever get into football again, be sure you own 51% (or more), so you are the boss!"

Now, the Brown family are principal owners of the Cincinnati Bengals!

Our families are friends forever!

Changes were happening everywhere!

Jane and Harry Leitch "called it a day" (as we used to say).

Harry's constant need for fun finally so outpaced Jane's capacity to endure it that something had to give!

Two examples are paramount:

Harry's enjoyment at being "over-served" led to a New York business dinner at the Cattlemen Restaurant.

Jane had accompanied Harry during a visit with Vince and Sally Costello. (He was the No. 50 middle linebacker – originally with the Cleveland Browns, now with the New York Giants.)

After dinner with the Costellos, who dropped Jane at the Cattlemen to connect with Harry for a late-evening flight back to Cleveland, Jane assessed the scene at the restaurant.

Harry was never going to make that flight!

He gave her her ticket to Cleveland and said, "I'll see you at LaGuardia Airport."

Jane went to *empty* LaGuardia – her plane was at JFK! She had twenty minutes to taxi to Long Island. The airline called ahead – "Hold the flight!"

An airline official was waiting – "Are you Mrs. Leitch? Hurry, hurry! I'll lead you to the gate!"

The pilot and crew were all waiting outside the plane!

"Please, Mrs. Leitch, your husband refuses to take his seat and is disrupting the passengers!"

Jane encounters Harry, and maneuvers him to a seat next to her!

He refuses to sit next to her, heaves himself to his feet, and decides to visit the cockpit – as the flight delay has caused Flight 153 to lose its rotation for departure.

When Harry returns, he throws himself into the aisle seat behind her, and the Hispanic couple next to him begin a very heated complaint! (In Spanish)

He calls the stewardess and demands a bigger safety belt – his is way too short! As the flight attendant tries to adjust his seat belt, it is discovered that Harry is sitting on the Hispanic couple's three-year-old son!

It was Jane's last trip with Harry!

A few months later, Harry wants Jane to accompany him to Cooperstown, N. Y., for Early Wynn's inauguration into the Baseball Hall of Fame. Jane and Lorraine are good friends from Early's visits to the Farm in Ft. Myers from his home in Nokomis, Florida.

Jane sends Billy Leitch – fourteen – and a huge baseball fan!

Billy is thrilled, and Harry has his life-long desire to play professional baseball rekindled when he encounters Casey Stengel – now with the New York Yankees.

Harry calls Jane!

"Get the guestroom downstairs ready for Casey and Edna Stengel. They are coming home with Billy and me for one night."

Unbeknownst to Harry, Mary Dana has left Elmer and is living in the downstairs bedroom – with all her worldly goods – just since Harry left for the week at Cooperstown.

Jane, Tim and Hal – and all available Leitches – begin emptying the guestroom and preparing for a once-in-lifetime adventure with Casey and Edna Stengel.

They have 24 hours!

Harry has called Bob August, Sports Editor of The Cleveland Press.

"If you want a great interview with Casey Stengel, come right over – he's here now." (And he was!)

Sitting in our family room were Casey, Edna, Jane, half a dozen Leitches, and Harry – who was in Seventh Heaven!

Casey was heavily leaning his elbow on Edna's thigh while he talked – non-stop – for two hours!

When Edna pleaded exhaustion – and asked to be shown to the guest room – she couldn't get up! He leg wouldn't hold her, and she fell to the floor.

Casey kept talking, and Tim Leitch rushed Mrs. Stengel to the nearest Emergency Room – thinking that she had had a stroke! Official diagnosis: Paralyzed quadriceps from unusual pressure!

After breakfast, a taxi was ordered for the airport, and Mrs. Stengel – noting that a severe rainstorm was happening – asked if she could borrow a raincoat, as she declared, "never to be returned!"

She was just Mary Dana's size! The last we saw of Casey, Edna, and the raincoat was the hem hanging down as the Stengels rushed through the rain to the waiting taxi!

At Jane and Harry's divorce hearing, the Judge read Harry's bios.

The Judge said, "Mr. Leitch makes all kinds of money, he's very successful, and his hobby is a spotter for the Cleveland Browns." With envy, the Judge sputtered, "Why, he's, he's, he's…"

Jane interrupted, "He's a 'legend!' Next time, *you* marry 'the legend!'"

The Judge declared, "Divorce granted!"

Actually, Harry *was* a legend!

He was the least boring person alive. As sick as he was, he never stopped working or supporting Jane and the six children and doing amazing things!

Jane just couldn't handle his powerful personality. And Harry's last words, "You're not going to spoil my fun!" seemed to say it all!

In the first two months (November and December) of Jane Sutphin's marriage to Harry Leitch, she learned what partying "Harry style" was all about.

He had accepted every Christmas party on the west side during the holiday season in 1950.

Returning to their one-bedroom apartment on Madison Avenue after another night of parties, Jane rushed to the bathroom and retched! ("No" to drinking; "yes" to expecting a baby in July.)

Harry shouted, "You have just ten minutes to get ready for our next party!"

With a cold towel held to her forehead, Jane violently shook her head and kept at the toilet bowl!

"You're not going to spoil my fun!" Harry shouted as he left the apartment.

Twenty-two years – and six children later – they were returning from a very long Cleveland Browns football game and the after-game party at the Cleveland Hotel – hosted every home game by Harry for all Browns players and guests.

It was 11 p.m.!

Harry said, "You have ten minutes to get ready for a party now (at Jim Graner's house)."

Jane shook her head, "No."

Harry shouted the fateful words, "You're not going to spoil my fun!"

Jane filed for divorce the next afternoon!

A few years later, Jane went into real estate classes at John Carroll and employment at Hilltop Realty, with a great boss, Vince Aveni, owner/director of Hilltop's residential sales.

Later, Jane was with Hackett and Arnold – and gave it all up to open the Spa in 1977 in Ft. Myers.

Before leaving the real estate world, Jane listed and sold Cal and Sandy's home on Lynn Park Drive in Cleveland Heights.

It had been home to our Sutphin grandparents, Gaga and Sutton. When they moved to the Farm in Fort Myers, Florida, the single Sutphin siblings, Mary E., Jimmy and Cal (and sometimes Pete Brown, Paul and Katie's son) lived there.

Our parents had sold Berkshire Road in Cleveland Heights and lived just blocks away at the Alcazar Hotel.

Cal had realized his dream in spades! He and Sandy had purchased an antique landmark, called "El Monte" – former headquarters of a Civil War general in Ellicott City, Maryland.

Cal had opened Braden Sutphin's second branch, and became a leading salesman in the Baltimore/Washington, D.C., area!

Their 10,000-square-foot house now housed seven nifty kids – Sally, Cal, Jr., Julie, Allison, Mia, Michael and Caroline!

Cal, Jr., still works for Braden Sutphin Ink in Maryland. Cal, Sr., President, retired on December 31, 2013. After brother Jimmy Sutphin became Chairman of the Board in the 70s, he retired in the 80s, and joined NAPIM (National Association of Printing Ink Manufacturers).

He and brother, Cal, received the Ault Award – highest honors of NAPIM – in the ensuing years.

Cal, 77 years old and newly retired, is writing a book on the printing ink industry in Washington, D.C., from his home in Ellicott City, Maryland.

**LESSON: THE ROAD LESS TRAVELLED IS NEVER CROWDED!**

Jane sympathizes with anyone writing a book. She knows this challenge as she shares, now, the 1980s, 1990s and the 21st century with you – and all her schoolmates!

# CHAPTER VII

# THE 1980S

Several major events in the 70s now took an "end run" in the 80s.

Jimmy and Cal Sutphin harbored very different directions for the future of Braden Sutphin Ink!

It caught us off guard! We had a *united front* mentality!

We believed that since all of us started as teenagers in the shipping room, we had a common goal. We practiced cash flow and low overhead, product development, and great personal customer service.

When Jimmy became Board Chairman – so that Cal could become President – it was understood that Cal, now married, would continue to live in Cleveland and operate out of Braden Sutphin headquarters at Aetna and E. 93rd Street.

Cal, however, envisioned his own branch in Ellicott City, Maryland – opening a whole new territory in Washington, D.C. – near Sandy's family, who were all scattered around Baltimore, Maryland.

With the company president in Baltimore, decision-making became more difficult – and reaching a consensus, even more so!

Eventually, Jimmy asked to be bought out!

The four Sutphin sisters thought of their Champ, who would have issued orders, calmed the waters, and pulled a rabbit out of a hat!

Jimmy joined the staff at NAPIM (National Association of Printing Ink Manufacturers) as Assistant Executive Director, becoming Executive

Director after two years. He remained there until retirement in 1997. He received NAPIM's highest honor, The AULT Award, at that time.

Jane was about to do her own end run and hat trick.

Jane had met Nathaniel Narten at a neighborhood brunch – hosted by Tom and Dindo Paterson – on Sheridan Road in South Euclid.

Harry had already moved to Lakewood, where he had been born, educated, had deep roots and many friends.

In the same year, Mary Dana and Elmer had made Jane a first-time grandmother – ready or not! Albert and Mary Sutphin were now great-grandparents.

As it turned out, "ready" meant custody of the beautiful little blond, brown-eyed doll, named Heather Anne Fisher. Mary and Elmer had done "the 70s thing" and disappeared.

Jane's three sons were on their own – Tim in college, and Hal and Bill in their own "digs."

Katy, 12, and Margaret, 9, had become Heather's big sisters.

Jane discovered that having bottles and diapers again – when divorced and seeking a new identity – rocks a very leaky boat! Many a lonely mile lay ahead.

Two years later, Nat Narten did his kind-hearted best to find distractions – and interesting friends – to keep Jane going.

In winter, Thursday night paddle tennis at Mayfield Country Club was a treat. (Jane's poor skills stood alone among those very good and experienced players who had been friendly opponents for decades.)

Nat's children (son, Spike, and wife, Janet; daughter, Suzie, and husband, Tom; and Chris and wife, Debby) gave Jane another family with growing children – helping her to feel connected.

Imagine the challenge of finding an activity that Nat – in his 60s – would enjoy with Katy (now 14), Margaret (11), and Heather (2 years old)!

One enchanted evening comes to mind!

With Katy and Margaret at camp for two weeks with best friends Josie and Nancy Lahr, Nat suggested an adventure that even Heather, at two, could enjoy – a ride into the countryside, dinner at a fun Drive-In, and a country auction at a famous old landmark in Medina, Ohio.

Heather is intrigued! Dinner provided a surprise gift – a flashlight on a key ring for our door at Heathermore!

Wandering among the auction items beforehand made it possible to assess the condition – and possibly find a treasure we weren't expecting. Nothing too promising appeared as we took our old-church-pew seats.

As the auctioneer took charge, Heather announced that she "had to go!"

Returning from the proper outhouse – a country-only adventure for Heather – we could not spot Nat in the crowd.

As he spotted us, he stood and waved frantically. The (now-animated) auctioneer shouted, "Sold to the man in the plaid pants!" Nat was now the proud owner of an enormous ten-drawer men's dresser – missing two drawers, as well as one of the four feet!

It seemed that a terrible scene would ensue if Nat refused to take it.

Heather was now jumping and laughing as we forced the monster into the open trunk and tied the door down.

Heather looked forward to *another date* with Nat!

Jane looked forward to finding a job!

When just out of college, she had sold advertising for a newspaper, called The East Side Shopper, at E. 105th and St. Clair.

The neighborhood was in transition in the 1940s – from all Irish to all Jewish merchants. To name a few, there was Khon's Furniture, Schreibman Jewelers, Izzy's Delicatessen, and, further west, Fish's unpainted furniture. There was also an Irish Catholic Church (and all-day Bingo).

Using them as references, Jane took her former skills to The Trader – close to Chagrin Falls and near Jane's present home in Moreland Hills. Without a sitter, Jane took three-year-old Heather along. Just as Jane was about to ask what salary the job paid, Heather fell out of her chair.

In mutual desperation, they hired her!

When Heather turned two, Jane was involved in something that she considered a miracle.

For *years*, worried sick about Mary Dana, Jane was on a frantic search to somehow get information about runaways, which was happening too frequently in the 70s.

Her search led her to an automobile that was parked way in the back of a McDonald's at Green and Mayfield Roads. She left a message – through a partially opened dark window – with her phone number attached!

A call led Jane to a house in Cleveland Heights, where a strange man told Jane where to find Mary. She was in the basement of a house where runaways were sheltered. The strange man was a NARC – short for a Federal Narcotics Agent – who kept constant surveillance on these young, lost souls!

Mary D. came home and reunited with two-year-old Heather – who sobbed and laughed and sobbed again when she saw her mother and realized who she was!

With Harry and the boys gone two years earlier, Jane, three daughters, and a granddaughter moved to a condo townhouse to economize/downsize. It was called *Heather*more – that name certainly rang a bell!

Jane later took Real Estate classes at John Carroll University. Nat joined her there, and upon graduation, Nat went to work for a competing real estate company.

They were friendly competitors until Jane left real estate to open the Look of Genesis Spa in Ft. Myers. Nat joined her there to run the business end of the Spa.

In the ten years that Nat and Jane dated – after Mary D. returned to care for Heather and to be a big sister to Katy and Margaret – there were adventures that dreams are made of.

A ski trip to Zermatt, Switzerland, found Jane high on the Matterhorn, where their passports would take them down the back side into Cervinia, Italy, for lunch and back again for a five-mile run to Zermatt's main street – to ski right into the hotel ski salon.

Then, dress for dinner and find dancing and music everywhere – having been delivered by a sleigh and kept warm under fur robes! All arrangements were made by Bud Davis and Nat's paddle buddies!

Next, the Alps and Kitzbuhel, Austria, and scenes of Innsbruck, where the Winter Olympics had been held, and a delicious cheese fondue – shared with a much-loved Laurel classmate, Janet Brookhart, married to Paul Jones.

Later on, Bud Davis (and his daughter, Stephanie), in his own plane, flew them to a Dude Ranch in Montana for a week. Jane starts imagining that this life must be for real!

"What's next?" Jane asks herself.

To Jane and Nat's mutual amazement, they were married on January 3, 1983, at Mayfield Country Club, among their children and Nat's life-long friends.

Heather had already cooked them a perfectly delicious engagement dinner the week before the ceremony.

At eleven years old, Heather became Nat's favorite dancing partner at the wedding.

Judge George McMonagle somehow didn't tie the knot tightly enough. It soon began unraveling – to Jane's distress and contrary to Nat's valiant efforts.

Jane forgot to ask herself if being married again would awaken old wounds. It seemed that knots tied in a Catholic ceremony – even thirty-three years earlier – were life-long knots which left scars and doubts when severed!

All over again, the pain of driving Harry out of their children's lives haunted her!

She should have told them how damaged she felt and how hurt she was that they would remember her only as a very angry, unapproachable mother!

Slowly, Jane realizes the life that Nat loved – and was born into – was not real to her.

It had been a ten-year odyssey without the lessons Jane needed to learn!

Ten years of days and places and people who had not filled the emptiness – through no fault of their own or their kind efforts. It was wrong not to love Nat in the only world he could recognize and be comfortable moving forward!

Later, Nat finds his way when he marries his best golfing partner and dear friend, Barbara, who sees him through happy rounds of golf, some health divots along the way, and many special events, with their blended families.

Jane realizes that "picking up the pieces" is the answer for her. Reconnecting with her children and siblings is her way forward.

The mid-80s finds Jane, her five siblings, and their 85-year-old, marvelous mother together in Ft. Myers.

For several years, they all have taken turns spending two weeks on the Farm, enjoying their mother's good company. She has had the companionship of three fine caregivers – all great friends – who spelled one another as needed.

At 80 years old, she had had emergency surgery for a blocked large intestine. A very young surgeon gave us no hope of her recovery – citing her age.

She breezed through intensive care, then a brief stay in a private room, avoided a nursing home, and lived five more years on the Farm.

She had survived 52 years with The Champ – old age was a slam dunk. Her legacy was huge!

She had given an only child, Albert, six healthy children – who had expanded his horizons immeasurably.

She had learned to cook hasenpfeffer (rabbit), Dutch sauerkraut, hot potato salad with extra vinegar, and wilted lettuce; and she baked many lemon meringue pies.

She earned an outstanding reputation for her baked beans (soaked overnight), with lots of brown sugar and molasses. They became a staple at every Braden Sutphin cookout and at every Cleveland Arena investors' party.

Those beans kept all our family, salesmen's wives, and other employees happily overfed when we gathered to address 5,000 Christmas cards every December at the Braden Sutphin plant (then located on Chester Avenue). Mom's baked beans were followed by the best ice cream ever – frozen in fancy shapes and pastel colors. A big favorite was the pink strawberry Christmas bell!

As a wife:

How many marriages would have weathered the unprecedented borrowing of $1,000,000 in the worst days of the Depression, to be paid back at the rate of $60,000 a year, as well as the six children who needed to be cared for, fed, housed, clothed, and educated?

How many wives thrive on guests who stay ten days at a time, eat, sleep, and then play shuffleboard and gin rummy every evening until 10 p.m., at which time a snack is served?

And star in their own original stunt on Poem Night?

How many wives are still smiling – and mean it – after thirty-four years of guests – from 1940 to 1974, January first to late April?

There were new arrivals every two weeks – sometimes twenty. Among them were sports figures, employees of Braden Sutphin, business friends, and family – all housed in the guest quarters. Others were year-round residents in the homes and the apartments on the property.

Our Sutphin grandparents lived on the Farm year round. Their home on Lynn Park Drive in Cleveland Heights was now occupied by bachelor girl Mary E. and her two single brothers, Jimmy and Cal.

Mary E. is housemother often. She welcomes Pete Brown, a student at University School. (Pete is the son of Paul and Katie Brown, who are spending the winter on the Farm in Ft. Myers.)

At dinner time – at 4 p.m. – our mother often greeted fifty and seventy guests.

For the first ten years, our mother ran the kitchen with two wonderful cooks, Ruth Knight and Mary Bailey. After Mrs. Galvin promised to "try out," she stayed for more than 40 years as manager. Guests, too, loved helping out.

Who would do all this?

Who loves this much – and so cheerfully?

The lady with the rosary! That's who!

Our mother and father took sharing, and engaging with others, to the level of an art!

The morning of November 13, 1985, our mother began packing!

It was Mary E.'s turn to visit. She inquired, "Mother, are you going somewhere?"

She replied, "We've had a wonderful time together, but I'm way overdue to visit my only sister, Florence. She's been gone thirty years, and I've missed her every day! I'll need a little lunch for my journey."

Mary E. prepared a little lunch!

Our mother said Grace, enjoyed her lunch (with her oldest daughter), put her head down next to her plate, and went to visit Florence!

Visiting Florence was a journey into a very nostalgic past.

During the Depression, as a young mother of three (two boys and a baby girl), Florence's life had taken an unusually dramatic turn. She had contracted tuberculosis!

Her husband, Dwight Walker, had an equally unfortunate turn. He went broke! As a builder – in a flat economy – there were no new homes being constructed. He faced a daunting decision. His brother and sister-in-law, Al and Mary Sutphin, offered to take the children until Florence had recovered.

For Mary, it was heartbreaking to imagine her beloved sister in a county sanitarium. Her children – housed and separated in Villa Angela, even a Catholic orphanage – was just too much!

Dwight's injured pride took over! The children went to Villa Angela Orphanage.

Florence lived away for three years, recovering from drastic lung surgery where all her ribs were removed (the known cure in the 1930s). Florence never sat upright again!

Our mother had prayed all her life for a "happy death."

She had a few aches and pains – but no pills! She lived 89 years on this earth, and now she knew a "happy death" when she saw one! Seeing Florence again was everything to Mary!

We have been blessed to have known the family saint!

Schoolmates, enjoy reminiscing as the 1990s unfold.

# CHAPTER VIII

# THE 1990S

As the Cleveland Arena and the Braden Sutphin Ink Company are Albert and Mary Sutphin's finest hours in Cleveland, so, too, is their Braden Sutphin Farm their finest Ft. Myers hour!

Both illustrate forty years of Al and Mary's driving energy, riveting foresight, a life-long caring and sharing with others, and the love they felt for each other, and the places they called home!

In 1977, Albert and Mary Sutphin had seen their $1,000,000 dream Arena torn down.

Nick Mileti had come into Cleveland like a whirlwind, bought the Arena and a mansion in Gates Mills, and renewed memories of his John Adams High School years and his Bowling Green University days. A nursing home on Cleveland's west side also figured in his past.

Soon after his arrival, he went into competition with his own property – the Cleveland Arena – by building the Coliseum in Richfield, Ohio.

Every important event – hockey, basketball, ice shows, entertainers – were now showcased in Richfield, nearer to Akron, Ohio.

As the Cleveland Arena sat empty, so did the purpose for its existence.

Mileti wanted the city of Cleveland to buy the Arena!

George Forbes, City Council President, held a serious grudge against Mileti for locating his Coliseum so far from downtown Cleveland. George Forbes declared, "No sale!"

Nick Mileti then gave the Cleveland Arena to Bowling Green University for a write-off!

His days in Cleveland seemed over for fun and games.

California called! However, a Mileti generation still exists.

His son, Jim, has a restaurant on Cleveland's west side.

## LESSON: THE "END OF AN ERA" CAN BE PAINFUL!

A remaining and loving memory about the Arena needs to be shared.

Spanning all of Champ's years was his friendship – in business on the Farm and in poker nights – with pal, Joe Gideon.

His J. C. Hub Printing Company was just one door away from Al Sutphin's early employment – as lone salesman – for the Braden Ink Company on E. 22$^{nd}$ Street in downtown Cleveland.

By answering his printing ink needs, Al Sutphin makes a great customer of Joe; and Joe finds himself a big believer and investor in the coming Cleveland Arena in 1937.

Fast forward to the 1990s, where the Arena image breathes one last time!

A 50$^{th}$ anniversary has been planned for the old Sunday Morning Arena Skating Club.

Jane Sutphin, married to Harry Leitch, will attend with great pleasure! The ladies are favored with a beautiful long-stemmed red American Beauty rose upon departure.

Something clicks in Jane's memory bank! (For some unexplained reason.) She has déjà vu of Joe Gideon and his wonderful Irish wife, Helen, who kept everyone laughing at all Arena events!

Helen is a widow, now, living on Lakewood's Gold Coast, and missing Joe every day.

Jane, busy tending six children, realizes that it has been many months since a visit, but the image of Helen simply takes over. Jane has to see her – now!

Jane begs Harry to visit Helen, taking the red rose! As Helen opens her apartment door, she falls apart, screaming, laughing and crying, as she pulls them into the living room.

It seems that she has been battling melanoma skin cancer for months. She needs to know if she will die of it! Catholics often pray for a "sign."

Helen has asked for a "red rose" if she *isn't* going to die of cancer (a yellow rose if she is).

Jane arrives with a *red* rose!

There are now drinks all around!

Helen buys a new mink coat and a new Cadillac car!

To her delight, her favorite sister calls – at Thanksgiving time – to invite Helen to spend that holiday in Las Vegas.

She knows that Joe would want her to go! She has more fun than she ever imagined, leaving herself seriously under the weather.

By Saturday, her sister has called the hotel doctor. As they wait, Kathleen is holding her hand, when Helen closes her eyes. She dies! The autopsy confirms a very rare Asian flu, with no known antibiotic.

Helen is with her beloved Joe Gideon! Her sister is wearing a nearly-new mink coat and driving a Caddy with only 1,500 miles on it!

LESSON: ALL'S WELL THAT ENDS WELL!

As we write of Al and Mary Sutphin's legacy, we find ourselves once more at their Ft. Myers retreat.

Our mother had died in 1985 in the house that Champ had designed for them. The Farm had become a landmark in the region and was known, facetiously, as "Munchkinland."

Much "nightclubbing" had led some young guests to be followed back to the Farm from Ft. Myers Beach.

The simple one-story houses with low-slung roofs led the revelers to imagine that tiny people – like Munchkins – were running around the grounds and in and out of the little houses.

The name, Munchkinland, had stuck for forty years! It's now a legend; and most old Ft. Myers residents, who have never been guests, believe it!

Not knowing how much time our remarkable mother had, Mary Dana and her five-year-old, Heather, stayed on after The Look of Genesis Spa had closed.

This gave the very first great grandchild a chance to enjoy the daily "soap operas" with three other generations – Gramma Jane, her mother, Mary Dana, and matriarch, Great Gramma Sutphin!

As our entire Sutphin seniors – by the 1990s – were buried at Colonial Gardens in Ft. Myers, we began realizing that none of the remaining family were destined to take over.

Bob Leitch and Carolyn had purchased a retirement model home at Parker Lakes in Ft. Myers.

Jane now occupied one of the original row-house apartments (#8) on the river. Several oldest and dearest friends had formerly lived there in its heyday. Now, #8 represented the last accommodations with electricity and plumbing! Jane lived on in what was now "Jurassic Park," according to brother-in-law, Bob Leitch.

All vegetation was once again starting to be roped together.

Washingtonia Palms had osprey nests way up on narrow tops. Late afternoons became the time to watch the osprey dive from the top, grab a fish out of the river, and return to the top to crunch every particle – nothing was left!

The raccoons, after trying to feast on anything else, preferred Jane's lonely garbage can – taking off the bungee cords with deft fingers and finishing with a drink from the swimming pool.

Bob and Carolyn's son, Rob, had married Clevelander, Kathy Murman, on the Farm; and were Farm managers until time ran out.

They stayed in Ft. Myers, and Kathy is the owner and manager of an outstanding Montessori School. Rob designs kitchens for large-scale, top hotels and restaurants.

Another son, Jeff Leitch, had contacted two close Cleveland friends, who joined him – as partners – to clear and then sell all as home sites.

The houses would be razed!

It is fitting that Alberta Sutphin and Ray Stoney would be in the driveway – on the Farm in 1992 – when the last occupied house was dismantled.

The furniture from the Sutphin family house was being loaded into a van to be taken north.

Alberta and Stoney watched the van disappear down the famous Royal Palm drive and through the gate.

The razing began the next day.

Carolyn Sutphin Leitch – who had made herself available for all family projects – was instrumental in negotiating the sale of everything of value in the seven homes and fifteen apartments on the last days of the Farm.

As she worked her usual long hours, she worried us!

She allowed cigarettes to become more important than food, and grew alarmingly thinner and greyer!

An operation at the Cleveland Clinic revealed a very large tumor, covering both lobes of her lungs. She had two months to live!

We five remaining siblings – forever engaged in one another's lives, and having to share this devastating news with our 28 children – were left a changed family!

The next generation, The Baby Boomers, were now front and center in our planning for the future!

Harry and Bob Leitch died within five years of Carolyn's death. Once again, cigarettes and *a few too many* contributed to this sadness.

Jane was now the oldest living Leitch, and amazed to realize how important Alcoholics Anonymous can be in a family's life. Even more amazing, it brought on a whole new reality – it was why she believed in God! Alcoholism is, and always has been, an illness – not a character flaw!

## LESSON: HAT'S OFF TO DOCTOR BOB AND BILL W.

New Year's Eve, 1999 – the last weeks of December – left everyone speculating as to a disaster of the Internet when the millennium changed from the 20th century to the 21st – with all those new zeroes: *2,000!*

Jane faced New Year's Eve alone. Remembering her talk with son, Tim Leitch, when he was *eight* – in 1959 – Jane, at 34 years old, had said, "Guess how old I'll be on New Year's Eve, 1999, Timmer? I'll be 75!"

He registered amazement!

Jane responded, "Oh, yes, and you'll be *50!*"

Well, here we were – 50 and 75!

Timmer had saved the date and the evening!

At 50 years young, oldest son, Tim, and wife, Bonnie, had invited Jane – 75 years, even younger – to a banquet of shrimp cocktail, filet mignon (rare), and Baked Alaska at their home in Chagrin Falls. *Her date* – their only son, and Jane's grandson, was 19-year-old Michael! Jane was home by 9:30 p.m. to watch New Year's Eve everywhere across the world – even China, at 6:00 a.m.!

The 21st Century is upon us.

Welcome to a new millennium coming right up!

# CHAPTER IX

# THE 21ST CENTURY

On the night of Braden Sutphin Ink's 100th anniversary – October 14, 2013 – we, as a family, had come full circle with our own destiny.

We were sharing the Cleveland Historical Society with Euclid Beach's famous carousel. It stood fully restored, a gorgeous reminder of our childhood fascination with Ferris wheels, "rolley" coasters, taffy and popcorn.

Through the glass walls, just beyond the dining tables set for 200 Braden Sutphin guests, we witnessed our favorite childhood recreation – come together, as partners – with our family's life-long dedication to the Cleveland ink industry. Both had formed us – creating a "feel-good" world.

In 1929, Albert and Mary Sutphin began their fateful journey toward ownership of the Braden Ink Company.

It commenced with a monthly check for an undisclosed amount – made out to James A. Braden. After his untimely death, the "mystery" check was made out to Mrs. Eleanor Braden, widow of James A. Braden.

According to one version – told early on by Al Sutphin – he continued to send the check to Mrs. Braden until her death at 92 years young.

Another version, reported when the Arena was sold, was that he was able to pay off the balance of his Braden Sutphin Ink debt with the $75,000 returned from his $25,000 original investment in the Arena.

Another version: Al Sutphin paid the second mortgage off on the Sutphin family home.

The family was aware of only two outcomes. No one has ever known the amount on those years of checks sent to the Braden family; therefore, no one knows how much Al Sutphin paid for Braden Ink – even Al Sutphin said he didn't know!

He announced that he was "debt free" after the sale of the Arena, and that sounded wonderful to his expanding family, who were finding ways into debt all on their own.

Braden Sutphin had many headquarters, all in the city of Cleveland.

For Al Sutphin – one of Braden's first employees – it was the fifth floor of the Vulcan Building at Ontario and St. Clair Avenues.

He was hired as a general worker, making letterpress ink, and selling from a push cart on every floor where a print shop existed.

As his cart emptied, he returned to the fifth floor, made refills, and started his route one more time.

After a move to the Caxton Building and the same routine, Braden Ink located in their own building on E. 22nd Street.

The first four little Sutphin children – all girls – remember it well.

Dad Albert would give Mom Mary a break. On Saturday mornings, he would take the four little girls to the office.

While Dad was busy in the plant, Miss Ziecheck, office secretary, was coping with Mary E. (8) on the typewriter, Jane (6) pasting stamps on envelopes, Carolyn (4) drawing pictures with the ink pad, and Alberta (2) making phone calls – to no one in particular.

The next move was groundbreaking – literally!

As the Arena was going up at 3700 Euclid Avenue, so, too, was Braden Sutphin Ink – back to back at 3600 Chester Avenue.

Brother, Cal, remembers, "Dad would work all day at Braden Sutphin, then walk down the driveway to the back door of the Arena and work all night!"

At this point, "The Ship" became a big part of Sutphin Family history.

As Braden Sutphin was being constructed on Chester Avenue (behind the Arena), Al Sutphin "got an idea!"

Architects were called in to design and construct a living, breathing *ship* on an upper floor at Braden Sutphin Ink. They would cover all four walls with canvas – floor to ceiling. The top half was a painted scene of a perfect seascape. The bottom half was a painted deck railing for looking out to sea.

121

Engineers had made it possible for the sounds of the sea to be heard as the walls moved – creating the ship's motion.

It saved a lot of money on food and booze, as one drink sent you sailing.

The "Ship" became famous as a party center – after Arena events and ink parties. Mary and Al knew how to do things despite the economy. If you couldn't afford elaborate food, everyone dressed up in fancy costumes and theatrical makeup and became a completely different person for that one night. The costumes dictated your behavior and provided your own fun.

When our parents were young and preparing for one of their evenings out, the four little girls piled on the twin beds and watched the fun.

Out came the cylinders of Stein's theatrical makeup, kept in a wooden box. They would paint one another appropriate to the period of their costume – Elliott Ness and Al Capone and their molls were popular. Dad would zip Mom into her costume, often a slinky long dress. Mom would adjust his tie and vest.

After the Arena was sold in 1949, Braden Sutphin Ink remained on Chester Avenue until 1957, and so did the ship.

The present location at 3650 E. 93rd Street has had additions – mostly in 1998.

Letterpress inks dominated the industry before 1960, with Web offset appearing around 1970.

Letterpress inks had amounted to 98% when Cal joined the industry in 1960. Cal had come home after a Ft. Myers High School graduation in Florida and found himself in a very familiar lifestyle at Braden Sutphin Ink's shipping room.

Cal had first-class ideas. He automated and modernized our old work space.

Now, roller-bearing pathways zipped all those 60-lb. crates directly to the delivery trucks waiting at the loading docks inside the building.

No more lifting and lugging as done by his sisters twenty years earlier. (The two boys should have been born first!)

As printers began putting in small Litho presses, Braden Sutphin Ink grew with them. In 1992, the company built a new 45,000 sq. ft. web heat-set and forms ink manufacturing facility in Carlisle, Ohio. Offset inks were now having their day.

As the 21$^{st}$ Century arrived, water-based inks were on the scene, followed by digital inkjet inks developed in 2007.

## LESSON: DIVERSIFICATION IS THE NAME OF THE GAME.

"Every success is found in the people!"

As the Sutphin family members began in the shipping room in the late 30s with four young sisters, they were followed by brothers Jimmy in 1948 and Cal in 1960.

If you came to work for the Braden Sutphin Ink Company, the following would happen:

You have a high school diploma and you live in the Miles Park area and you are looking for work.

In 1958, you would walk several blocks to 3650 E. 93$^{rd}$ Street and apply for a job.

If you were serious about working, Braden had this to offer you:

1. A choice of three shifts: day, swing, or night.
2. If you stayed a year, you were eligible for the Pension Fund (every dollar you put in was matched by the company).
3. If you continue to show up, you have a job for life if performance matches attendance.
4. You now can expect a yearly bonus and 100% of your health coverage paid by the company.

Many of the underprivileged in the neighborhood become the plus-30-year veterans – the Danny Browns, the Jesse Hightowers, the Bill Dabneys, and the David Wrights.

And – not from the neighborhood – the John Biotonis, the Jerry Nunnallys, and the father-and-son team, Carl and Jay Shaffer. Another team featured a mother/son combo, Bev and Michael Schwartz.

Michael's wife, Patty, was a granddaughter of Patsy Callaghan, a Cleveland Baron hockey player, who, in retirement from hockey, gave the remaining thirty years of his life to management of the Braden Sutphin factory office.

A bit of history: In the 30s, you will find that ink was delivered by motorcycle, with your order in a sidecar.

Everyone worked until noon on Saturdays! When World War I was over, Al Sutphin might have stopped to see Joe Gideon, next door at J. C. Hub Printing, and then continue on one more door to Central Electrotype to see what Mary Hoynes was doing Saturday night.

For forty years, technological innovations were in the very capable hands of G. L. Erikson – called "Tiny" for being 6'4" and 250 pounds. He was Braden Sutphin Ink's longest plant manager – and an extraordinary chemist. His non-scratch half-tone black revolutionized the letterpress industry, making Braden Sutphin Ink a leader. He was "given the nod" during WWII, and offered his services to his country for $1.00 a year for the duration.

Taking his place in R & D (research and development) was John Ritzic, who became a magician with the customers who ran into trouble – often in the middle of the night. They could count on John Ritzic – sometimes driving hundreds of miles – to the rescue.

Ted Zelek was an original success story. Al Sutphin had noticed Ted playing a very good game of basketball for John Carroll University on those special Friday Doubleheader Nights at the Arena. He backed his education by giving Ted odd jobs at Braden Sutphin until he graduated. In his fifty years with the company, he rose steadily from shipping room to manager to CEO and finally to Chairman of the Board.

Another very beloved forty-year veteran was Tom McManamon. He came to Braden Sutphin Ink from service in WWII. All during the war, his indispensable wife, Jane, excelled as the Champ's secretary. Albert Sutphin sent Jane home to start a family and hired Tom the minute that WWII ended.

Tom was managing a dozen different jobs at the Arena when it was sold in 1949. He immediately became an ideal manager at Braden Sutphin Ink and rose to Chairman of the Board.

At the Arena, he had been Al Sutphin's right-hand man, a great counsel and go-to guy. At his death, Tom became a lovable memory. He was a Dad to four sons, with one of our family's best-friends-forever wife, Jane.

Braden Sutphin has emphasized service to the ink industry, as well as long being active members of NAPIM.

Jim Sutphin joined NAPIM in 1989 and served as its Executive Director from 1991 to 1997.

Albert Sutphin and sons, Jimmy and Cal, received the organization's prestigious Pioneer Award. Mr. Erikson, Mr. Zelek, Mr. Ritzic, Dan Neese, and Byron Hahn were also honored. Jim and Cal Sutphin and Mr. Erikson were recipients of the highest award in the North American ink industry, The Ault Award, bestowed through NAPIM.

The Sutphin third generation (the Baby Boomers) are well represented: Cleveland CEO, Jim Leitch; Michigan Branch Manager, Matt Stoney; and Virginia's Senior Branch Manager, Cal Sutphin, Jr. Tim Leitch, Gail Stoney Viccelli, Ray Stoney, Jr., and Jamie Sutphin are all involved in sales.

CEO Jim Leitch, with Braden Sutphin Ink since 1989, had this to say:

"With the competition fierce, it will take a leadership team and employee group that is just as fierce. Braden Sutphin has been meeting that challenge, and will continue to do so going forward. We have seen our position strengthened by staying committed to being a partner with our printer clients. We believe this will be the cornerstone as we begin the next 100 years!"

The present Chairman of the Board, in this very modern and diversified era, is a steadfast supporter of all things Braden Sutphin.

Jim Krost's blood runs cool and competent in ways of being a progenitor. He is a Braden! He stands alone, among three generations of ink-drenched Sutphins, by selling insurance when he isn't "at the Board." He is everyman's "neutral corner!" (As in boxing.)

(Jim and Eleanor Braden had two daughters, Bunny and Eleanor. Jim Krost is Eleanor's only son.)

A favorite long-time employee is John Paderewski.

The Champ and our mother lived at the Alcazar Hotel, beginning in 1955, and a trio of weekend entertainers took their fancy. Jan Paderewski (John's grandfather) played piano while his mother, Kay, sang, and his father, George, played organ and accordion. Every great tune of the 30s, 40s and 50s were their specialty.

When the Paderewskis (Jan, Kay and George) left the Alcazar to build their own "Paderewski's" at Lee and Harvard, our family were frequent attendees.

John aspired to a business-oriented life. He joined Braden Sutphin Ink, and for 30-plus years, has been a quality control manager. Though trained in piano and trumpet, he now plays the Spectrophotometer and the Inkometer.

He adds two delightful stories to his family history!

John Paderewski's grandfather, Jan, taught Liberace to play the piano, having spent many years in Las Vegas, and became famous as a virtuoso at the piano and as a piano teacher with extraordinary talent.

John's own personal story involves an historic encounter with his famous grandfather, Jan.

As John turned four, grandfather Jan challenged John.

"Young man, our family of musicians now have covered the piano, the organ, the accordion, and singing, but no one plays the *trumpet*. In what instrument may we start training you?"

Four-year-old John answered, "The guitar!"

Balancing a male-dominated industry, and much appreciated, are women with 30-plus years on the front lines for Braden Sutphin Ink:

Debbie McCloud, Order Entry and Billing Manager.

Pat Soto, Accountant for Receivables.

Secretaries:

> Irene Zbydniewski, former lab technician and outstanding Editor of the Braden Sutphin Ink "News-O-Gram" and in Purchasing.
> Betty Nagy, retired long-time secretary to Jimmy Sutphin.
> Noreen Kolokowski, outstanding Executive Secretary for twenty-five years.

Michigan became the very first branch in Braden Sutphin Ink's 63-year history.

When Ray and Alberta Sutphin Stoney returned from managing The Farm in Ft. Myers, Ray became a salesman for a long-established territory in Michigan in 1962. By 1970, Ray had become a natural at making people feel good about buying Braden Sutphin Ink.

In 1971, turning a sales territory into a branch meant that mixing and blending proofs, color matching, and lab work would be accomplished in Michigan.

The ink manufactured at Cleveland headquarters would be shipped by bus to Detroit. Without a building, ink was soon stored in the Stoney basement, the garage, and even the car.

Ray, Jr., and twin, Matt, were soon old enough to cover outside sales with their Dad and inside office management for the branch.

Their oldest daughter, Gail, after a meaningful career with Tupperware, joined her twin brothers and took over inside phone sales.

Following Albert and Mary Sutphin's lead, they soon did a great deal of entertaining – and business boomed!

Gail set sales records inside, while "the Rays" (father and son) did the same outside calling in the territory. Matt was now office manager – making color matches, etc.

They had become the standard bearer for the seven branches that followed.

Ray, Sr., was making a very big name for Braden Sutphin Ink.

ISO, standardized certification for the auto and other industries, became a task that was handled by Gail for Braden Sutphin Ink's Cleveland headquarters. The Pension Fund was another! So was Board duty!

Alberta, not to be left behind, grabbed her rubber gloves, mops, pails, and detergents and kept everything spic and span.

Three more little sisters at home, Ann, Lynn and Elaine, were recruited for duty when ink parties were often planned. They had taken various jobs directly from high school and have worked ever since graduation day, almost forty-five years ago.

Gail, Ray, Jr., and Matt have approximately forty-plus years each at Braden Sutphin.

The graphic arts industry, featuring country-wide litho clubs, are well attended by all Braden Sutphin managers, and honors keep falling their way.

Benjamin Franklin's birthday in January is always cause for celebration. For many years, a very formal dinner dance was held at an important Cleveland landmark; and it marked the start of the long winter social scene of concerts, lectures, sleigh rides and ice skating parties.

Mary E., as the oldest and leader of the second generation to enter Braden Sutphin's work force, was the first to leave – after all her sisters were married. Her last duties were revamping and redecorating all the public areas and offices at the present location on E. 93rd Street and Aetna Avenue.

She was an inspired leader – a carbon copy of our Dad, the Champ, and fiercely independent. She needed her own identity.

As her five married siblings began having their 28 children, she was inspired to create "Little Folks," which became a highly successful children's shop which opened in 1965 at Cedar Center. After ten busy years, it became a fabric and yarn shop.

The Champ commented, "Mary E. fell in love with her inventory – didn't move it enough – fatal in retail."

He was often right, but it brought former nurse girl Betty Cook back into our lives. She had married John Moran, now happily employed at Braden Sutphin Ink for forty years.

Betty herself was a fantastic needle-woman. She taught many a novice knitter or crocheter to find their own success, as did Mary Margaret Struven Lynch, trusted partner and Laurel School friend.

Mary E. could never deny herself a chance to build something. It led to a wonderful fixer-upper year-round cottage on the water at Put-in-Bay, Ohio, on South Bass Island. It overlooked Perry's Monument.

After fifty years, her friendships included everyone on the Island.

The original cottage was partnered by three life-long friends. They called themselves the "Four Quarters." Jack Schwarber, the only guy, was a popular decorator from William Taylor Son & Co. in downtown Cleveland on Euclid Avenue. Marge Alge, society editor for the Cleveland Press, Hilda Miller, a good friend, and Mary E. rounded out the group.

As Mary E.'s many nieces and nephews became visitors every summer, her pals were happy to buy her out. Mary E. then turned her talents to a complete renovation and expansion of an adjoining property. It had been a real estate office, but contained three bedrooms and two baths.

Otto Herbster, a well-respected photographer on the Island, allowed her to tear down an old barn of his. She used the lumber and the talents of an old friend, the experienced and talented John Yarish. Together, they enlarged the kitchen and added a living room and an office. Eventually, a big porch and a large ramp to a lovely yard and revamped garage, complete with upper-floor living quarters, were added.

Sister Bertie and Ray Stoney became so intrigued that they were now – for many years – the owners of a year-round house on the East Shore.

They added seventeen nieces and nephews, who grew to love island living, and kept the Jet Express busy from April to October.

Mary E. now had a "tent town" in her yard and phone numbers handy for all public sleeping accommodations on the Bay.

The Stoneys had been wonderful neighbors and close fun family for decades. They palled around almost every day, and "their gang" helped and loved Aunt Mary, who was known for telling them to shape up!

As Mary E. neared fifty years on the Bay, she was wearing out. Alberta and Ray realized that she couldn't be alone.

Enter another niece, so far away in Sarasota, Florida, that she wasn't considered a "regular."

Jane and Harry had a free-spirited daughter, Mary Dana, who, at 45, got real, and became a very capable end-of-life RN, very skilled in nursing the sick and dying! Mary E. was in perfect hands for the month she had remaining.

In July 2004, she was air-lifted off the Island to Hillcrest Hospital in Cleveland where most of her family could be with her. Her nephew, Jim Leitch, her Executor and CPA, was arranging for Mary E. to be transferred to Hospice of the Western Reserve.

As evening approached, her two oldest and closest friends, Mary Schloss and Jeanne Gaul, gave her their usual high-spirited attention. It was the ideal send-off. Mary E. died – after they left the room.

She was in perfect peace with a lifetime of well wishes and one-of-a-kind accomplishments to her credit!

Braden Sutphin Ink's 100th anniversary was coming within the decade. Her family is sure that she had a front row seat!

Jane was now the oldest Sutphin, as well as the oldest living Leitch.

A slow realization began to take over her usual casual thoughts. Has Mary E. somehow passed the mantle? Is Jane more a presence than she has ever imagined herself?

The Sutphin family is huge, with over 130 progeny – many living in Cleveland, some in Michigan, and others in Baltimore.

Is Jane a commanding enough personality to signify leadership, or have years of taking a fun-and-games position established her as a lightweight?

As she reflects, she knows – for certain – who she is. She is the witness to the soul of a family!

Money, for money's sake, was never even imagined. It was only to give a gift, share a place, be a friend, do a good deed, dream a big dream, and believe in God!

Jane has spent a lifetime saluting the printed word, the four-color press, the inspired carton and label image, the annual report, and the gifted people who made it all happen.

She had been encircled by parents who knew how to nourish and lead, provide stimulating challenges and good clean fun, and belief in a higher power.

She was surrounded by siblings, who told her the truth, supported her endeavors, shared the real facts of life – get yourself educated, be a good and wise friend, lend a buck when needed, and have the time of your life, because you are rarely alone.

Jane has six children- forming the fourth generation- who all know how to work, who care about others, have frequent get-togethers, discuss golf handicaps, March Madness, the Browns, the Bengals, the Indians, the Cavs, and who has the clicker?

The fifth generation- from forty-two-year-old Heather to nine-year-old Liam Burns- are a work in progress. Part of that work for Heather is playing mother-of-the-groom for son, Matt- of the sixth generation when he marries a beautiful school teacher named Jennifer Loman. Matt's sister, Kristen, is a guest and twelve-year-old Julian is a groomsman in 2014.

There is a rumor that a seventh generation will appear on September 15, 2015. EXTRA EXTRA EXTRA The Sutphin family proudly welcomes: CAIDEN ROBERT ERNST the first of our seventh generation. Born on August 28, 2015, in Dunn, North Carolina, to first ever Great Great Grandmother Jane Sutphin Leitch.

As a family, when we looked back:

Past lesson: The days don't dim.

Present lesson: They speak, and we hear violins – it's magic.

Future lesson: Life is not a photo op. It is a journey over hot coals, where one learns to dance a lot.

Thank you, God!

# EPILOGUE

Thank you, dear classmates, for sharing our journey and learning our lessons together.

"Our Champ" always reminded us that Braden Sutphin Ink would "loom large in our lives – making all things possible!" We would meet interesting people, have goals to achieve, and create a product to send out into the world that will make a difference.

It will make a college education possible, awaken your children to horizons beyond our own universe – a family together in purpose!

Only future generations can imagine the importance of "The Moondog Coronation Ball," originating at the Cleveland Arena on March 21, 1952 (and closed after one number for overcrowding – 20,000 tickets printed and sold for 10,000 seats!).

Alan Freed had coined the phrase, "rock and roll" on his WJW radio show. Now, rock and roll was the new cultural phenomenon influencing lifestyle, fashion, attitude and language!

The Cleveland Arena had led the city one more time into the history books – and, this time, into the future as well.

With further love and gratitude for:

Timothy Brownell
Mary Dana
Harry Albert (Hal)
Billy Brady
Katy Jane
Margaret Lindsey

*Jane Sutphin Leitch*

My children are porcupines; their quills are fragments of me!

Blessings always,
Your Mother,
Florence Jane Sutphin Leitch

Those who were sent to me!

Gratitude to all those who made possible, through their interest and assistance, an unforgettable series of images that found their way from my pen to the written page.

Lou and Jackie Groza, whose belief in family and "the Game" was an inspiration that fostered loyalty in friends and fans for more than fifty years- on the gridiron and in my heart.

Rusty Brown and husband, Bill Tanner, one a columnist, the other a reporter and former Managing Editor of the Cleveland Press. They are a gift to the creative process!

Rusty, now, as a writer and performer of historically fascinating women, Bill, her manager (when not writing for local newspapers in Ft. Myers, Florida). They inspire excellence in all fledgling authors.

Family members: my Tim, Mary Dana, and Katy Jane, who shared the burden of a surprise heart attack (midway through nine months of writing) to keep me going – with the constant support of my Hal, Billy, Margaret, and Liam, and spouses Bonnie, Barbara, and Bonnie, who put a "memoir" above all else!

Sandy DiAngelo Sutphin, brother Cal's wife, who set sail my creative juices by constant encouragement (called badgering) that worked!

Sandy Jones, valiant typist, whose tireless dedicated belief in a new author's family tales kept us all going!

Julie Liedtke, Julia Doyle, Kate Merlene and Anna Benedikt, worthy researchers at Orange Library in Pepper Pike, Ohio.

Marisue Besse, good neighbor at Heathermore (Moreland Hills, Ohio), an early "finder of info" on her computer.

Chris and Warren at Kredo Hardware, where I bought three dozen pens (a month). (Warren courted his wife at Cleveland Arena events in the 60s.)

At Braden Sutphin Ink Company, Tim Leitch and Angela Castillo. Irene Zbydniewski and John Paderewski, Info and Copy Editors.

Les Roberts and Dan Coughlin, long-time great writers, and my idols.

Dr. Scott A. Wagenberg and staff at Hillcrest, who gave me new corneas, so I could write a lot!

Dr. Jonathan S. Scharfstein at Cleveland Clinic, who fixed my ol' heart to write and love another day.

Our Special thanks to good folks at LuLuPublishing

Finally, when you are looking for " Partners in Crime," look no further than your double cousins: Jeff and Jan, Rob and Kathy, Carolyn and Dick C, Jim and Diana, Dan and Colleen, all dear, good Leitchs and one very special Castele!

Amen!